DOG TRAINING & BEHAVIOUR

Geoff Grinham

The Crowood Press

First published in 1994 by
The Crowood Press Ltd
Ramsbury, Marlborough
Wiltshire SN8 2HR

British Library Cataloguing in Publication Data
A catalogue record for this book is available from the British Library.

ISBN 1 85223 751 1

Picture Credits
Line-drawings by Gillian Gray
Photographs by Geoff Goddard and the author, except where it is stated
otherwise. Photo on p. 31 by Croft Engineering, Wigan WN3 5BD
(tel: 0942 497677)

Acknowledgements
Many people and dogs have helped over the years to fine-tune my dog
handling ability; they will always be remembered and appreciated for
their tutorship and the pleasure they have given: Khaki, my very first
Airedale Terrier; Squire Gubbins, for teaching a 'Town Boy' Country
Ways; Ted King, for all those fishing trips with dogs and for saving my
life; Dave Waghorn, my best Army Pal; Lt.-Col. Wright RAMC, the best
Commanding Officer ever; RSM Bongarten; RSM Cambell; Tom and
Jerry, Airedale Terriers remembered for their prowess at catching
thieves and rabbits; Roy Hunter of the Anglo-American Dog Training
Academy; Wendy Volhard, for the Long Down and Aptitude Testing;
Croft Engineering, Wigan WN3 5BD, for supplying me with their canine
equipment; Sylvia Barnes of local Farnborough fame, for her patience
and tolerance; Kelly, Angela, Harry and William, my present gang of
Airedales; Ken Monkou, who appears on the back cover, Airedale Terrier
owner and close family friend; my sons David, Stephen and Peter; and
last but far from least, Margaret, my childhood sweetheart and dear
wife, for her forbearance during the past forty-two years.

Typeset by Acorn Bookwork, Salisbury, Wiltshire
Printed and bound in Great Britain by BPC Hazell Books, Aylesbury.
A member of The British Printing Company Ltd.

Contents

Preface

Having a well-behaved dog reflects the character and status of the keeper. Unfortunately, in modern society numerous political, legislative and animal welfare agencies acting in unison produce a wealth of misinformation based on human logic, which, in some instances, makes responsible dog ownership a heavy burden to bear.

Man has used dogs for centuries in a host of working roles in peace and at war. Today, all over the world family dogs compete in a wide variety of canine sports, work as farm dogs, protect property, help police and other law enforcement agencies, entertain punters at race meetings, perform cabaret acts, make hospital visits, and perform a multitude of other duties.

Scientific fact confirms that humans are much more intelligent than dogs. Familiarity and experience in training and working with dogs, however, bring into focus a completely different definition of intelligence. Dogs are clever capable creatures, probably much more in touch with the peaceful green essentials for survival on this planet than the human race will ever be.

Certainly, in modern times, man has failed horrendously to understand animal welfare. Looking at life from a dog's point of view, the human race qualifies as the most ignorant species this world has ever produced. Strangely though, to qualify as a good dog person, you must have a liking for people and enjoy human company.

The first step towards understanding dogs is dismissing the myth that an old dog cannot be taught new tricks. The second is that there is no such thing as complete obedience, especially with regard to dogs. Dogs are not by nature obedient creatures, but fortunately, with a little understanding, they are easily controlled. Control not obedience is the goal for a companion dog.

Hopefully, the chapters in this book will help both experienced and inexperienced people new to dog ownership to reach a deeper understanding of dog behaviour and training, with the desired side-effect that their dogs may enjoy greater fulfilment as human companions.

God grant me the Serenity to accept the things I cannot change, the Courage to change the things I can, and the Wisdom to know the difference.

Anonymous

PART 1
CANINE DEVELOPMENT
AND PSYCHOLOGY

CHAPTER 1

The Language of Dogs

Whilst dogs do not have the power of speech, they are able to communicate using body language: facial expressions, tail movement, head and ear carriage and various vocal sounds combine to form an effective means of communication. They receive information by sight, sound, touch, taste and scent.

Between the ages of four and seven weeks, puppies learn they are dogs and to communicate with each other. They play a variety of instinctive games with their litter-mates, hunting, mock killing, steal-ing, games of strength and dominance. The seven-week-old puppy will have learned a host of communicative skills; all its mental faculties will be well developed, and he will be, relatively speaking, highly experienced. The only thing required to build on these founda-tions is more experience.

Puppies removed from the litter at too young an age may never learn they are dogs; in some instances, this may lead to antisocial behaviour towards others of their own kind. On the other hand, a

'This is the life!' A litter of contented four week old puppies taking their fill from the milk bar.

Three mischievous five week old puppies plan their next foray.

puppy going to a new home after the age of twelve weeks may develop too primitive a character.

Pet dog owners make a very big mistake when they treat a small puppy as an infant child. The child may be helpless; the puppy is far from being so. From day one in a new home, a young puppy is well able to find its feet and to modify human members of the new pack to suit canine comfort and ideas of pleasure, most of which may not be conducive to human domestic bliss. To begin with, the puppy will primarily be interested in who sleeps on the highest territory and who eats first. Using eyes, ears and nose he will quickly learn if the establishment has a vacancy for a worthy pack leader. Adult dogs going to a new home can take up to eight weeks or more to show their real character and establish social rank. Timid mature new arrivals, may, over a period of weeks, turn out to be overbear-ing characters, requiring continuous supervision on a day-to-day basis.

The advice of many authorities is that puppies should not be trained until the age of six months. Whilst allowances have to be made for the fact that a puppy does not focus its mind on any single thing for more than a few moments, it would be foolhardy to delay its learning for so many months.

Discipline

The most important fact of life a puppy must learn before departing from the litter is to accept discipline. Dominant puppies deprived of this essential early learning often become difficult dogs to live with.

When a litter of puppies is well established on solid food, the dam is taken away and her rations reduced to dry up her milk. She then spends two, two-hour periods each day with the litter. On her first return visit to her progeny, all the puppies charge for a feast at the milk bar. The dam waits for the right moment – when all her teats are occupied and the pups least expect it – and then she leaps at her varmints, snapping and snarling viciously. The puppies run off in various directions in a state of shock; they momentarily take stock of the situation, then herd together, seeking safety in numbers. Mum approaches the litter, and then licks and nurtures each puppy in turn. Most have learned through the psychological principle 'shock followed by reward', and their behaviour changes after a single experience; the milk bar is permanently closed. Sometimes a hyper-dominant pushy puppy will try for a second attempt at the milk bar. The moment its lips touch a teat, the demeanour of the dam becomes intense.

She grabs the offender by the throat, pins it to the ground and feels for any sign of submission by the puppy. Submission is rewarded by licking and maternal nudging. Puppies subjected to dam discipline in this way normally respond well to human requirements when passed on to their permanent homes and are willing to accept human leadership.

Punishment

Dogs behave in accordance with instinctive and conditioned response patterns. They associate pleasure or displeasure with their memories of day-to-day living, and avoid repeating unpleasant experiences and seek to repeat pleasurable events. Punishing a dog for not coming when called will certainly imprint an unpleasant association in his memory, with the result that the sin will be repeated.

Dam (mother bitch) disciplining one of her puppies in no uncertain manner.

This six week old puppy has lots to investigate: shrubbery, toys, wasps and a host of other new experiences, some pleasurable, some not to be repeated.

Preceding a reprimand with the dog's name can cause him to ignore the name on future occasions. Another classic example of canine thinking is that the pleasurable experience resulting from thieving the Sunday roast may override any fear of punishment; the sinner will learn to use cunning to avoid blame next time.

Nothing useful can be taught to a dog by using punishment. Doing so indicates a complete lack both of knowledge and the power of command on the part of the trainer. When you own a dog you are totally responsible for its well-being and behaviour, to the extent of having the power of life and death. This responsibility should not, therefore, be taken lightly, and it is essential that your dog never has cause to doubt you.

Admonishment and reward must be well timed if a dog is to learn and benefit from them, as it is essential to associate them with what is actually in the mind of the dog at a given moment. For example, all a dog resting on the settee is thinking about is peace, quiet and rest. Telling him off in this situation will not create respect for the trainer. If this happens a few times the dog may regard the arrival of the owner as an unpleasant event, he will not blame the settee. However, if he is admonished at the exact moment he starts to climb onto the furniture – while he is thinking of the sin – then admonishment is justified and purposeful.

Repetition

Basic control exercises, Sit, Stand, Down, Stay, Dog's name Come and Dog's name Heel, are learned through repetitive experience. Dogs have a twelve-hour memory bank regarding new repetitive learning. Consequently, during the early sequences of training the best policy is a little and often. Session training should be delayed until the dog or puppy has established a happy playful association with control discipline and training.

Obviously, the dog must learn to respond correctly to single commands, such as 'Sit', not 'Sit, Sit, Sit'. Nagging will teach him that he does not have to comply unless it suits him to do so. The correct response will not go into his permanent memory until he associates at least two inducements with each basic command, one visual and one sound, normally by voice or whistle and hand signal. Once the command is in his permanent memory, he will respond to either inducement. However, if both inducements are not on occasion used together, over a period of months the association can be lost and the dog will become detrained.

Motivation

Motivating a dog to learn requires nothing more than common sense. Anyone can teach a dog to sit for a biscuit, but such bribery does little to teach control. The sit response for food is, in fact, a mechanical response, not a control procedure, and results from the fact that if a treat is held above a dog's head he must look up and back slightly, which is easier if he sits. Reward is, of course, an essential ingredient, and during learning sequences of training it is important to be lavish with praise when the dog responds correctly. Care must be taken, however, not to praise when he fails to respond or becomes distracted.

Unintentional Training

Many examples of undesirable dog behaviour result from unintentional training. One of the most common of these is jumping up at people. Owners coming home after some hours of absence are immediately given a warm welcome by the family dog, who jumps, claws, sniffs and licks: undesirable behaviour probably taught on day one, when the whole family could not resist rewarding puppy approaches with petting. Stretching out hands to repel the onslaught makes physical contact, thus rewarding the undesired behaviour. It is much better to ignore excited conduct completely and walk past the dog as quickly as possible. A moving target is much more difficult. Not only does absence of reward contribute to erasing this problem behaviour, but the dog is also made to feel unwanted for a few minutes, thus imprinting in his memory an unpleasant

First impressions suggest a loving relationship full of compassion, but this needs to be kept in check until desirable behaviour disciplines and basic control are established.

association with the behaviour. He learns, by experience, that his trainer does not respond to over-excitement.

Another example of unintentional training concerns fearful responses. Reassuring a dog or puppy when it displays fear rewards what is actually in its mind at that moment, resulting in the conditioned response, 'Mummy only loves me when I'm nervous'. One example of this may be a dog refusing, through fear, to follow his handler on lead through a doorway. Force should not be used in this instance; instead, sufficient lead tension must be maintained to prevent the dog backing off, leaving him with only one option, to advance. Given a little time and patience, necessity will override fear; the instant it does so, a huge reward is called for. Consequently, courage not fear is reinforced.

Summary

Dogs learn by the association in their minds of pleasant and unpleasant experiences. Allowing a dog to take an inch gives him much pleasure and, very quickly, the inch becomes a mile. A dog's interpretation of good and evil is that if he gets away with a sin, it is good, if he is caught in the act, it is evil.

CHAPTER 2

Critical Development Periods

Post Whelp Period (Birth to 12 Days)

The early neo-natal first twelve days are concerned with only three body requirements: food, excretion of waste and warmth. If these essentials are not provided puppies will, in most instances, die. Unfortunately, the heat-regulating centre of a puppy's nervous system does not fully function until about the third day. The litter are absolutely dependent on the dam for warmth, nourishment and the removal of excretory waste, including keeping rectums clean. Warmth is, in the main, provided by the litter bunching together and insulating each other. Contrary to the requirements of the litter for warmth, the dam needs to keep cool.

Neo-natal puppies are blind and deaf. The senses of smell, taste and touch, although present, are unpractised and need experience to become efficient. They move by crawling in straight lines to locate the dam and in circular motions to locate their litter-mates.

The only emotion a neo-natal puppy can show is stress related to discomfort. Stressed puppies cry perpetually in a high-pitched tone until the cause is relieved. Contented litters are quiet, apart from the odd deep-sounding grunt or squeak.

Transitional Period (13 to 20 Days)

Eyes open at the beginning of this period and mark the onset of other physical changes. The ability to see, however, does not develop until the twenty-first day. Movement gradually progresses in stages. At first the puppies are able to crawl backwards as well as forwards and, after a few days, develop the ability to stand and walk in a rickety manner. The first teeth start to show on about the twentieth day, when the puppies begin to bite and chew.

Emotionally, they are able to show pleasure through tail-wagging, which is not triggered by sight or sound, although some response to vision and sound may be noticed on the last day of this period, representing a stage of very rapid physical development.

Within this brief period the puppy becomes able to hear, walk, perform body functions without tactile stimulation, keep itself warm and eat other than by sucking.

Awareness Period (21 to 28 Days)

Marked changes in sight and hearing

ability occur rapidly within a 24-hour period. Learning starts now and it is important that most desirable new experiences create a pleasurable mental association. First experiences of light and noise must be subdued, and sudden shocks must be avoided. Dependence on the dam and a stable environment become even more essential, as is gradual familiarization with human beings, male and female, adult and child. This is the period when a puppy begins to learn it is a dog and what being a dog is all about. Sudden environmental changes may cause permanent emotional weaknesses.

Canine Socialization Period (21 to 49 Days)

Now the fun begins, with the puppies becoming ever more active day by day. Although feeding and sleeping continue to be the most prolific behaviours, there are daily brief periods of high activity; much has to be investigated and learned by the adventurous puppies, new skills developed, especially body and vocal language and their effect on litter-mates and human contacts, the different meanings of tail and ear carriage, facial expressions, and a multitude of contrasting scents.

Numerous games are played during this period. The puppies generally play in trios and practise chase games, hunting and mock killing. During these games each learns just how hard they need to bite to cause pain and injury. They take it in turns to play the victim and predator. The victim yelps when sharp teeth cause pain, signalling it is time to switch roles.

A puppy's consistent success in the jockeying at feeding times and over the possession of toys earns it a high rank in the pack status and a position of dominance. Bitches are as capable as dogs of being pack leader, and some will become more authoritarian than any dog leader.

It is normally unwise to break up a litter before the age of seven weeks, and perhaps in some cases eight weeks. Doing so may have a drastic effect on the eventual adult dog character, making it anti-social to other dogs and humans. However, there are numerous factors which affect the rate of a puppy's development, including breed type. Puppies which are intended to become Guide Dogs for the Blind are sent to their foster homes at six-and-a-half weeks. Committed Obedience Competition handlers like to select and take home a puppy at six weeks of age. Experienced dog breeders of integrity know the best period to pass on their particular progeny to new homes and environments.

At seven weeks of age a puppy has learned a great deal, knows its potential social rank status, and, whether dominant or submissive by nature, has developed some skill at manipulating others, both human and dog, for its own benefit.

Human Socialization Period (7 to 12 Weeks)

This is the best age to introduce and accustom a puppy to a new environment. This may be conditioning to farm animals, motor traffic, noise, screaming, chasing children, the veterinarian, in fact, the big wide world.

There are two key factors at this stage in puppy development: immunization and the First Fear Imprint Period. Most vaccination programmes commence when the puppy is eight weeks of age and end at about fourteen-and-a-half weeks. Veterinary advice is to isolate puppies until the end of this period because of the risk of infection. The needs of character development, however, demand otherwise. Restricting a puppy to the home patch during this period will result in it not developing to full potential. This does not necessarily mean the puppy will become a bad dog, only that it will not mature to its full promise.

There are alternatives which in part satisfy both demands. Town dwellers can spend a few minutes with their puppy each day at the front boundary of their property, watching passing vehicle and pedestrian traffic, including mums with children and pushchairs, and other dogs. Many may stop to pass the time of day and this impresses on the young canine mind the message that such exchanges are normal and friendly, not intrusions.

Hatchback cars also represent wonderful opportunities for socializing young puppies. Sitting on the open tailgate for half an hour, two or three times a week, at public open spaces and shopping centre car parks, allows puppies to experience shopping trolleys, crowds, happy and upset children, and a variety of sudden noises in a secure and familiar immediate environment. Such experiences help to strengthen trust and respect between canine and human.

Hatchback cars are not the only suitable means of transport; the front carrier basket of a bicycle can be adapted to convey the puppy safely in a manner which allows it to observe outside events.

Towards the end of this period, consideration should be given to controlled exposure to experiences in the dark. Puppies may have a horrific first impression if such after-dark experiences are not introduced gradually. Flashing vehicle headlights can imprint absolute terror in a vulnerable puppy. Less vulnerable types may not see or realize that headlights represent fast-moving road traffic. Exposure must be based on the principle of a little and often. The manner of the tutor should be confident and convey the message that there is no cause for concern with a natural matter-of-fact attitude.

First Fear Imprint Period (8 to 11 Weeks)

Frightening or painful experiences have a more lasting effect at this age, than if they occur at any other period of development. This is not the best age to send a

Sudden shocks can have a marked, long-lasting effect within the First or Second Critical Fear Response Periods. Strange experiences should be avoided during this time.

puppy on a long journey by road, rail or air. Most airlines insist that a puppy must be over eight weeks of age for in-flight transportation. Puppies under eight weeks travelling on a long journey are prone to rapid dehydration, but, because of the First Fear Imprint Period, between eight and eleven weeks they are liable to form lasting phobias related to the means of transportation and possible incidents during the journey.

Puppy owners must be able to identify the marked differences between fear and caution. Caution in a dog is a very desirable trait. Walking through a doorway with a puppy or dog often creates a classic caution/fear incident. A fear response to this situation may be demonstrated where the dog retreats as quickly and as far as the owner and lead will allow. An example of a cautious response would be the dog anchoring its bottom firmly to the floor and refusing to advance any further. Both instances require patience, not sympathy, on the part of the handler, who should stand on the exit side of the doorway with sufficient lead tension to prevent the dog retreating backwards, leaving him only one option, to go for-wards. Time must be allowed for the dog to make the decision to advance of its own accord and, the instant it does so, liberal praise must reward the moment of bravery.

Rank Classification Period (13 to 16 Weeks)

This is the age at which genetically domi-nant puppies begin to develop confidence and endeavour to achieve high rank in pack status. There are degrees, ranging from mild to extreme, to which a puppy can, by nature, be dominant, whilst other puppies are submissive and require a completely different management ap-proach. Self-important dominant puppies require flattening, whilst submissive characters need a boost to their strength of character. This period of development is the best time to balance both factors without damaging canine dignity. In-depth supervision is essential. The domi-nant puppy, for example, should not be allowed to eat before human members of the household, or sleep on the highest territory.

Owners must establish themselves in the eyes of their puppy as leaders of high status. Doing so requires, by human social standards, a degree of meanness. For example, if a puppy is lying in a corridor and you wish to pass, it may be polite and convenient to walk round or carefully step over the pup. Such conduct signals you are puny, to be looked down on as of low rank. Making the puppy move out of your way will instil respect for your authority and pack leadership, and will also, after a few repetitions, teach him that it is not safe to rest in corridors or get under your feet.

Dogs are pack animals, whose instinct for pack survival overrides any degree of personal preservation. Pack instinct dic-tates that the family or pack *must* have a firm leader. In the absence of a person-ality they consider to be a competent leader, both dominant and submissive puppies and dogs adopt the responsibility themselves. The dominant become very overbearing and may attack and bite for any pack indiscretions on the part of their owner. Submissive puppies who take on the duties of pack leader find the respon-sibility extremely difficult and stressful and can easily become panic fear biters, lacking in the power of discernment between friend and foe.

Meanness is not an excuse for physical or mental cruelty. Firm handling during this period sets ground rules for a lasting and loving relationship. Control must be established during these formative weeks, and until it is, love must take a secondary role. It is easy to make the critical error of allowing compassion to overturn common sense, and falling in love with a bundle of cuddly fluff, which, of course, will grow up to be the finest dog and best friend anyone could wish for – or will it? Now is the time to make sure, using knowledge, commitment, common sense and, a great deal of good luck. The older a dog becomes, the harder it is to instil control, and love can so easily turn to hate and/or shame.

Although specialist puppy training classes have become the vogue in recent years for puppies of this age, it may not necessarily be wise to bring mixed breeds of similar aged puppies together in groups. The Cavalier King Charles of sixteen weeks may find giant breeds of thirteen weeks more than a little awesome. Size as well as age should be balanced at such classes, which are in theory an excellent idea, but in practice often leave much to be desired.

Proper socializing with other dogs is a priority at this age. This is best achieved by taking short on-lead recreational walks in the company of other dog handlers, who own well-behaved, socially acceptable dogs themselves, as puppies generally mimic and learn from their peers. A family's pet dog can have rather an exclusive upbringing, and care must be given not to spoil a good puppy for the sake of a little thought and effort.

Second Fear Imprint Period (6 to 18 Months)

The Second Fear Imprint Period is not as accurately defined as the first. Dogs grow in spurts between the age of six and eleven months and, at times, may appear to be out of proportion physically. Between twelve and eighteen months they fill out, becoming, in most cases, balanced adult dogs.

Individual dogs, even of the same breed and litter, can display different developmental patterns. Some demonstrate a Second Fear Imprint Period of about four weeks' duration; some display fear symptoms for a few days only at frequent intervals; others may at times throughout their life have days or weeks when they become easily spooked for no apparent reason. Each dog owner has to cater for the idiosyncrasies of their particular dog. Harsh admonishments during a fear response period can cause deep longlasting hurt to canine feelings.

Owners must be observant of behaviour changes in their maturing puppies. Perhaps a puppy has a set behaviour pattern for greeting in the morning, normally full of excited enthusiasm, but suddenly, one morning, a subtle change occurs and the puppy is timid in his approach; or perhaps instead of attacking his breakfast as usual, he is hesitant; perhaps the puppy barks at familiar objects – all are signs indicating the onset of this period.

Only the owner can decide whether it will be beneficial to take the puppy to a training class during this period. If previous class experience has been happy, then the puppy's attitude will be positive. Should his perception of class have a stressful association, it is best to avoid such situations. After all, a stressed dog

Members of Breed Dog Training Club preparing to give a public demonstration of canine control at a country fayre. As proof that older animals can learn, most of these dogs began training as mature specimens.

will not learn anything useful, but may develop a strong dislike for all group situations, human and canine.

Maturity (1 to 4 Years)

Dogs who lead an active working life mature quickly, although different people have various views and priorities on this score. Shepherds look forward to having four years of working experience behind their Collies before describing them as mature. Yet the same dogs compared to their domestic cousins are very mature at two years of age. Domestic pet dogs retain a degree of immaturity until well into old age. A sentiment often expressed to frustrated dog owners is 'Don't worry, they grow up when they are ten years old'.

The more we can teach a dog before it is a year old, the better. All the patience, tolerance, tender care and teaching of these twelve months form a solid foundation for more advanced training and understanding. What a waste if the learning experience of puppyhood is allowed to stop at maturity: it is fact, old dogs can learn new tricks.

CHAPTER 3

Rank Order in Pack

Man has, for centuries, bred dogs to serve a variety of practical purposes. Through selective breeding hundreds of breeds have been produced, with just about every possible contrast in shape, size, colour and character. Despite vast differences, all are capable of reproducing with the others. Each litter of puppies develops a rank well before their forty-ninth day and includes hyper- as well as hypo-dominant characters. Dog owners should have a deep understanding of how dogs identify social status.

Dogs have their own ideas on every aspect in life. It is not known how they came to be domesticated by man, although it was probably the dog's, rather than the man's, decision. Given the chance, a dog will take everything and give nothing back. Consider the question of who serves who in your household. Being servant to a dog is conducive neither to domestic bliss nor harmonious dog ownership. Compassion and sentimentality lead many people to believe that their household is not complete without a pet dog and/or cat. This is fine, provided one understands that kindness is not normally reciprocated by family dogs, and that dominant dogs need firm management by owners with strength of character and common sense.

This chapter describes how dogs learn their proper place in the social order of family life. Readers who have had a long relationship with their dog must be cautious regarding the advice given here. Sudden change in behaviour and discipline is dangerous. Character adjustments must be made gradually to achieve improved control over a dominant dog.

Pack Discipline in the Wild

Studying packs of wild dogs and their behaviour gives us an insight into how dogs identify rank. Pack discipline is strict and the pack maintains standards which are not permitted to decline.

When the pack are at rest, the leader always occupies a comfortable place at the heart of the territory; a position which may be at the highest elevation, or perhaps in the shadiest and coolest spot. Other high-ranking pack members surround their leader and keep close company with him. Next, but at a slight distance, come the mid-ranking members, who constantly jockey with each other and at times have brief physical encounters in an effort to elevate their rank. Finally, on the outer territorial perimeter, the puny dogs of low rank are allowed to rest. They are referred to as perimeter dogs, who eat last and are allowed no privileges. However, they play a vital role in pack survival.

Perimeter dogs are busy, neurotic characters, alert to every strange sound or incident in their environment, which they investigate with cautious concern. They give the alarm when danger threatens and will, if necessary, lay down their lives to protect the pack from predators. Should a higher ranking dog try to assist at such times, he will be driven back with considerable ferocity by the subordinates who, when their adrenalin is running, demonstrate completely contrasting behaviour to their normal timid conduct. Many a good dog has been mistakenly destroyed for attacking his owner in a highly charged situation, when in fact his intention was to protect and drive his superior away from danger. This is not an uncommon response in the field of security when, apprehending a villain, a well-trained dog sometimes unexpectedly attacks his superior for coming too close to what the dog considers dangerous. Although the demeanour of the dog may appear extremely aggressive, perhaps with teeth bared, actual physical harm is most unlikely if the warning is accepted.

These primitive instinctive traits still prevail in domestic circumstances, and so hierarchy is decided by instinctive canine behaviour patterns involving sleeping arrangements, play including games of strength, feeding, territory, possessions, interactive grooming, and reflex action at close quarters. Modifying canine dominance necessitates playing rank, using instinctive behaviour language a dog can understand in accordance with basic ground rules.

Basic Ground Rules

Rule 1

The dog is not allowed on furniture. Owners must decide where their dog will sleep. Should the dog be left to decide, favourite resting places will include the owner's bed, armchair, and the floor immediately in front of the fireplace or television set. In the family car small dogs often choose the rear parcel shelf because high elevation over others indicates high rank; with larger dogs the driving seat is the most likely place.

Rule 2

The dog's food should be prepared at the same time as the owner's in the presence of the dog, who must observe the owner eating first. The owner may need to pretend a hot drink is a banquet when young puppies are fed more frequently.

Rule 3

Play tug-of-war with the dog on-lead at the owner's invitation, *never* the dog's, for short infrequent periods. The dog must never be allowed to win or keep the play article. Tug-of-war is the only game of strength which should be played with a family dog. (Be very gentle with puppies.) On no account should you engage in hand to paw/mouth combat, or handle the dog roughly.

Rule 4

Possessions: the dog is not allowed to own toys, and can play at the owner's invitation only. Articles must be put away afterwards. Do not allow the dog to enact 'catch me if you can' scenarios.

Rule 5

Territory and the prevention of territorial

aggression. Walking a dog regularly at the same recreational area can, in some instances, particularly with high ranking males, cause serious incidents with other dogs or humans. Similarly, when attending training classes or other events on a regular basis, sitting or standing in the same location can lead to problems with dogs snapping at each other. The policy should be variety. This holds true even with the dog's bed; he must not be allowed to believe it belongs to him. Using synthetic washable sheepskins as dog bedding and occasionally using them as an extra cushion for your own armchair gives him the important message: bedding belongs to you, not your dog.

Corridors in and around the home can be a territorial problem. If a dog is lying in a doorway, out of politeness people are inclined to step over or walk round him. Repetition of this, with some dogs, leads to the situation where no one is allowed to pass without his consent and sometimes this consent is withdrawn. Always, from the very first, make him move out of the way with a firm command 'Get', thus teaching him respect for your high rank.

Whether a dog becomes territorial or not depends as much on individual character as on unintentional training. It is best to make sure though, by enforcing the territorial policy.

Rule 6

Power of command: all commands must be given with authority, touched with humour and a playful handler attitude, once and once only on each occasion. Do not plead or nag. Your dog understands 'Sit', but will never comprehend 'Sit, Sit, Sit, Sit'.

Rule 7

Grooming between dogs is a social behaviour related to pack survival and status. The higher rank grooms and in turn is regularly groomed by subordinates in the same pack, but always at the invitation of the senior dog. Similarly, regular grooming, at human invitation only, can have a considerable influence on how biddable a family dog becomes.

Experience indicates that aggressive incidents are more common with smooth-coated breeds, especially among pedigree dogs, than with long-coated varieties. Although many domestic pet dog owners believe their smooth-coated dogs do not need frequent grooming, and in aesthetic terms this may be true, it is, however, crucial with regard to rank and pack well-being. Family dogs need a regular daily spruce-up with brush and comb at the invitation of the owner to help keep them in their proper place.

Compliance with these rules is vital with dominant dogs. When your dog understands through practical everyday experience that you are quicker and stronger than he is, then, and only then, will he credit you with being more intelligent. When he does so, he will sit up and salute your every whim with great sincerity.

There are always exceptions to the rule; in this case, the shy subservient dog whose self-confidence needs boosting. Even so, do not deviate from the routine of eating before the dog, or be over-sympathetic to shyness, and still groom your dog for fifteen minutes every day.

Remember, do not enforce all the ground rules instantly if your dog has been in your care for some time. Make changes gradually.

A supreme example of Retrieve (Carrying) and purposeful Control.
(Photo: Inara Gorobets, Latvia)

Summary

Training a dog has more to do with controlling instinctive behaviour than inducing submissive obedience. A practical policy is to give human purpose to each behaviour trait. For example, if your dog has a strong possessive trait and is forever stealing shoes and slippers, it is easy to train him to fetch and carry items by their name, shoes, car keys and so on. Your goal must be to use such behaviour habits at the right time, in the right place, and at your invitation only.

CHAPTER 4

Temperament and Disposition

The word temperament is often misused when talking about dogs. Hounds and terriers, for example, have contrasting breed temperaments, but both should be of a social disposition which makes them acceptable company at any time or place. The term unsound temperament can be used to describe hounds with terrier temperament and vice versa. Socially attractive characteristics are influenced both genetically and by early learning experience. Sound dogs can be ruined by a single bad incident.

Training is another frequently misused word, as it is often interpreted as teaching obedience. Dogs are not obedient by nature, so trying to make progress in a dog training programme when thinking in these terms will lead to a great deal of frustration, adversely affecting both canine and human temperament. The correct word for training any dog is control, and it is the human partner who must learn how and when to control a student dog. There are no grey areas: either you have control, or you have lost control at any given moment.

Within canine circles the word obedience has a sporting definition and refers to competition obedience. Nearly every weekend in the United Kingdom thousands of dogs and their owners take part in such competitions, giving impressive displays of control in the competition arena. However, some competition dogs are absolute hooligans outside the arena. Pet dog owners require a more general type of control over their dogs to that demonstrated in sporting circles. The exactness of response to basic commands need not be technically perfect for pet dogs; however, speed and willingness to respond must be conditioned to levels of distraction greater than those of most competition arenas. Achieving such levels of discipline requires just as much commitment on the part of the pet owner, as the sporting competitor. Just being involved is not good enough. People who have an affinity with dogs, but do not have the inclination or the time to give the necessary commitment, do dogs a great service by deferring dog ownership until their circumstances allow them to make this commitment.

Why out of all the animals in this world has the dog become man's closest friend? Suitable temperament and disposition must be contributing factors, although the catalyst for compatibility of human and canine friendship is more complex. Intelligence must contribute as an attracting force, and although man is more intelligent than any dog, this is measured in a human environment. A solitary human, if accepted by a dog pack and forced to survive as a pack member, might develop a different understanding of intelligence. There are other more intelligent species which have not evolved as useful companions to man. Some of the ape family even use hand signals as a means of communication, yet they are not as attractive in temperament or as practical as the dog for sensible companionship. The most essential ingredients, therefore, must be intelligence and personality; ideally, not too intelligent but with plenty of personality.

Man identifies with mutual emotions in dogs, some good and some bad – jealousy, playfulness, mischievous behaviour, vitality, tolerance – and generally empathizes with changing moods. If there is one word to cover all the factors and idiosyncrasies which bond the relationship, that word is chemistry; and the chemical formula which creates a good relationship is unknown – you either have it or do not.

Developing a Sound Disposition

Being a dog owner means playing a major part in the formation of sound acceptable characteristics and behaviour in the adult dog. The end product is, in most instances, what the owner or trainer deserves; you cannot command success, only deserve it. Dog owners have a responsibility to society to ensure their success at being able to control their dogs at all times. Responsible dog owners are caring enough to cater for the needs of their dogs and sensible enough to train them not to be a nuisance.

Recreational walks present wonderful opportunities to develop sound disposition in our student dogs, to show them life through everyday events. Each outing may present new experiences: the first jogger, horse rider, cyclist, uniformed people, running screaming children, sheep, cattle, and other domestic animals. It is no use standing back and watching your dog's response to such new experiences. You must anticipate and intervene at the very first sign of erroneous behaviour, before the sin is committed. This way you avoid the need for correction, which in most instances is usually too late. Desirable conduct in the face of new experiences must be rewarded and not taken for granted.

How will your dog respond the first time he spots a pile of horse manure? His first reaction will be to roll in it and cover himself in the canine equivalent of an expensive perfume. Walking him away to avoid such offensive behaviour denies you the opportunity first to admonish and then to praise, thus teaching him that such behaviour is not acceptable. Walking deliberately towards the manure and, at the first sign of interest, sternly commanding him 'Leave', then praising when he responds correctly, will, after a few repetitions, prevent such obnoxious behaviour becoming a bad habit. Admonishment is not the instrument of learning, it only interrupts sinful behaviour; learning comes with the praise which must follow admonishments, when the dog responds correctly.

Many owners erroneously walk their dogs away from likely incidents, particularly from other animals. Animal instinct, however, tells the dog that retreating objects or creatures are, in general, fair game to chase and investigate or even attack. Walking away from strange dogs can give the impression that you want to avoid other dogs. Repetition of such events may train some dogs to be aggressive to others of their kind. Approaching joggers and other passers-by should be addressed with a friendly greeting, followed by a brief exchange of social conversation, thus demonstrating to your dog that such events are normal and friendly. Passing the time of day with other people in the presence of your dog does not mean you have to interrupt the walk. An interruption may, especially with an inexperienced dog or puppy, unintentionally induce over-excited greeting behaviour, or, in dogs who have a strong protection trait, unnecessary antisocial aggression. Should a halt be required for more familiar conversation, provided the dog has been taught to respond to the 'Sit' command at high levels of distraction, retaining control is simple. Your goal is to condition your dog to a disposition that is neither over-friendly nor unfriendly, with the added bonus of reinforcing his power of discernment of friend or foe.

Breed Temperaments

Terrier-type dogs are expected to have a game temperament, useful for controlling vermin such as rats and rabbits. Often, a terrier purposely bred for such duties is wrongly accused of lacking gameness when he allows rats to wander his territory with impunity, until one day an occasion arises when in a friendly manner the terrier approaches a cornered rat. The rat responds defensively by biting the dog's nose. Terrier gameness is immediately triggered, and, in an instant, a lifelong intense hatred of rats becomes implanted in his terrier memory. Killing rats becomes a conditioned response.

The necessary genetic ingredient for gameness should not depend on a strong kill instinct, but more on an innate dignity which is easily damaged. Many ignorant dog breeders deliberately rear progeny with strong inherent kill instinct and take pride in their false interpretation of gameness. Since the introduction of various forms of rat poison, such dogs in today's world are often displaced personalities. Public concern for a less toxic world may bring about an increased demand for game terriers to control vermin. Hopefully, new generations will have strong humility and dignity traits which will allow the kill instinct to be easily controlled.

Gundog temperament has also, in some instances, been drastically altered by modern breeders, sometimes not necessarily for the good. Essential inherent quiet gundog reserve has, in some cases, been exchanged for extrovert hyper-excitement. Blame does not rest solely with the breeders but also on the fickle tastes of the general public, some of whom have no knowledge of what makes a dog tick, but nevertheless hold strong opinions regarding what they think they want.

Mongrel dogs born as a result of natural canine rather than human selection, usually have a moderate mixture of basic behaviour traits and are neither over- nor under-endowed with particular instinctive temperament attributes. In terms of character most are well balanced and interact favourably with other dogs and people. Their conduct can generally be described as moderate for their species. Selective breeding to modify basic canine behaviour habits of pedigree dogs should have as its goal the improvement of social disposition as well as the enhancement of physical conformation.

Reading A Dog

Living and working with dogs over a period of time develops an ability to 'read' every dog, to see the soul at the point where nature triggered life to make it a dog. Sometimes, the ugliest mutt has an inner beauty which, at the moment of recognition, is strong enough to raise a tear of appreciation for his radiant dignity. Doing anything to damage such dignity is indeed a horrendous crime.

Most dogs have considerable scenting ability and can instantly identify human intentions and character by using their nose. Occasionally, when dealing with a problem dog, trying to modify undesired behaviour and establish a bond where trust is lacking, a brief moment comes when the dog first identifies with your own good intent and, in an instant, makes the decision to exchange mutual trust. While such moments are rare, they illustrate perfectly the capacity that exists for the meeting of the human and canine spirit.

Whether dogs have souls or not was a very topical subject among theological and canine literary publishers in the early twentieth century. While dogs do not have any sense of morality, reading a dog confirms that they do have souls and a great deal of heart and it is this knowledge that provides the power to motivate a dog during training to work *with*, not just *for*, you. Knowing the difference between with and for guarantees that dog owners are on the correct mental wavelength and will in due course receive many complimentary comments regarding the sound temperament and behaviour of their dog.

Aptitude Tests

Anyone anticipating ownership of a puppy or dog need not leave the personality of their prospective companion to chance. Aptitude tests have been long established and proven as a valuable guide for assessing canine genetic and inherent personality traits. Professional puppy or dog personality testers will, for a modest fee, select a suitable puppy for a potential owner. Both experienced and inexperienced dog people sometimes employ the services of a tester to minimize the risk of making a bad choice. Specialist testers within a particular dog breed will, in compiling their report, comment not only on the dam but on the stud, who may not reside at the same address or even in the same geographic area. Testers familiar with a chosen breed will know in some depth the common traits of previous progeny produced by an established breed sire.

Tests include a general analysis of the strengths and weaknesses in the areas of: pack instinct, prey instinct, defensive traits, dependence/independence, possessive instinct, sound, sight and touch sensitivity, fear, courage, intelligence, dominance, aggression.

Physical conformation – how closely to the classic breed standard a puppy is likely to conform – is fairly easy to determine between the ages of seven and eight weeks, but not so easy from ten weeks until near maturity, as the puppy grows in fits and starts. The end product depends as much on the future dog owner and environments as on the breeder. Many a potential champion has been ruined through dietary imbalance, over- or insufficient exercise, accidental injury, infectious disease, or lack of loving care.

Square pegs in round holes!

Idiosyncrasies of potential owners and their environment are also taken into account before making the final selection, ensuring that round pegs go to round holes. Vendor and purchaser sign a contract, including protective clauses for both parties. The tester advises on any adjustments needed to the future environment and management of the dog. Occasionally, a prospective purchaser decides that dog ownership is not a good idea, but remains appreciative of the tester's advice.

Summary

Many specialist dog breed books include terms such as 'excellent with children', 'friendly', or 'fun to live with' when describing temperament. This ignores the fact that in every litter some of the progeny will be good for nothing, others good for practically any reasonable environment, some will love children, while a few will hate youngsters. Do not be influenced by such facile generalizations. Remember that the relationship between dog and man is two-way and effort, friendship and common sense have to come from man if he is to own dogs of a friendly disposition and sound temperament.

Mischievousness, properly controlled, is a trait which can be an essential, if small, part of the pleasure of dog ownership. 'The whole world loves a villain', so the saying goes. Applied to dog ownership, it helps when they have a bit of spirit and an appetite for purposeful fun and games. 'That's my boy! Let's live, pal.'

CHAPTER 5

Canine Welfare

It requires considerable management skill to train a dog to full potential. Every decision has positive and negative side-effects when put into practice. Should Jack be castrated or Nel spayed? Should we buy a puppy or a mature dog? Pedigree breeder or rescue kennels? What age is the best to start training? What about holidays? Can we afford his keep? What breed type? Make no mistake, dog ownership is a luxury in these modern times.

Responsible ownership means being fully and solely accountable for the well-being of a family dog. While many owners accept this obligation with a moral sense of duty, some people treat their dog as an object, to be put aside until the whim takes their fancy. Dogs have feelings and a strong inner need to belong to a pack. Few can adapt to a human working week in which they have limited social contact with their owner Monday to Friday, and then at weekends receive too much attention and are perhaps exercised beyond their restricted level of physical fitness.

The first requirement of a caring owner is to 'think dog'. Doing so requires a forward outlook, on a wide spectrum of topics open to many permutations of result. Every topic relates to and has an effect on the next. Visualizing results necessitates 'joined-up thinking'!

Acquiring Your Dog

Obtaining the right dog for your circumstances and environment needs considerable thought and planning to avoid bitter mistakes. Those who choose a pedigree dog should not, in the hope of reducing the purchase price, inform a breeder, 'I only want it as a pet'. Such statements guarantee that you will be sold the runt of the litter. The advantage of selecting a pedigree puppy is, in many instances, being able to see the dam and perhaps the stud, which will give a good indication of the likely adult conformation and character of the progeny. Even if you have to pay a little extra for a good specimen of your chosen breed, awareness at the point of sale will be very cost-effective in the long term. Simply paying a high price, however, is no guarantee of quality.

Some very sound dogs come from animal rescue centres, such as Battersea Dogs' Home; such charitable establishments compensate for the inadequacies of irresponsible people, as well as for genuine previous owners. However, even rescued canine waifs can be quite expensive. Some centres have their regular 'boomerang dogs', who are a picture of sweetness and light until the moment you get them home! Boomer may then urinate on beds, door jams, and clothing, and can chew a hole in the refrigerator door with the velocity of an armour-piercing artillery shell and in no time consume the contents. Boomer's stay is a brief one and he is usually back at the rescue centre within forty-eight hours.

Genuine rescue dogs take up to eight weeks to overcome inhibitions and trust that their new home is permanent, and during this period their behaviour will change considerably. Separation anxiety is a common problem with many, though not all, rescued dogs. It seems that they instinctively know they have been saved from a horrific fate, or perhaps, through misfortune, they have become parted from previous loving owners. Consequently, they are excessively anxious that their new-found owner may be taken away. Living with such a dog, despite his perhaps very loving and companionable nature, is not easy. You are unable even to visit the bathroom without being escorted by the dog. If you go shopping without him you may return home to a scene of destruction, any item containing your body scents having been torn to shreds. Fortunately a great deal can be done from the first day to modify or prevent the anxiety becoming established. This is described in Chapter 22.

When taking on an adult pedigree dog, from any source, insist on a trial period of three months and do not let your heart rule your head during that period. Many dogs with serious aggressive traits are passed on either because the owners cannot bring themselves to have their pet destroyed or because they are too miserly to pay the veterinary fee. Put the sale-purchase arrangement in writing to avoid later misunderstanding or even, in the event of serious incident, prosecution under civil or criminal laws. This way you relieve the existing owner of their dog, but responsibility is shared between both

parties for a specified time and you are unlikely to be burdened with an aggressive dog, whose antisocial traits may not be evident until it is too late.

Purchasing a puppy has one very big advantage: being able to bring it up yourself and at the same time have full knowledge of its background. Most puppies are very lively creatures, and start life in an adopted home with their new family playing all the rough-and-tumble games learned with their litter-mates. Human skin is not as tough as a puppy coat and playful mouthing by needle-sharp puppy teeth can, in no time, cover hands and arms with marks.

Puppies must be house-trained. If purchased from a knowledgeable breeder, the puppy will arrive already house-trained and, provided you carry out the instructions given by the breeder, you will not have any problem with soiling indoors. If this is not the case, have a ready supply of old newspapers and an indoor puppy pen.

When you buy your puppy the breeder should give you an initial cover note for veterinary and third party insurance cover, its Kennel Club Registration Certificate (you must register the change of ownership), a detailed diet sheet, a signed copy of pedigree, a receipted bill of sale, and the date of the last worming and the drug used. Puppies over the age of eight weeks should also have a vaccination certificate. Many breeders do not bother to vaccinate puppies they intend to sell, thus putting financial gain before puppy well-being. If this is so in your case, find another breeder. There are vaccination programmes which can be started at six and a half weeks of age; common policy at most veterinary practices is to give the first inoculation at eight weeks.

The price of a pedigree puppy varies enormously from surprisingly little to a few hundred pounds. Whilst it is wise to avoid being seduced by an apparent bargain, paying a high price is not an assurance against a disastrous purchase. In general, though, you get what you pay for. A puppy is most valuable up to twelve weeks of age, after which, its value (although not necessarily its price) drops as fast as a new car leaving the show-room. This is because canine trust of, and dependency on, the human partner is most easily and quickly established prior to this age; early experience has a profound and long-lasting effect on a dog's attitude, so this is the best time to lay the foundations for a reliable and mutually satisfactory relationship. Having said this, adult dogs trained for a specific purpose and Show Champions command purchase fees many times above puppy prices. Making a wise purchase is, of course, fundamental to the future well-being of all concerned.

Naming Your Dog

This may seem a rather trivial matter, or at least one that is a question of no more than personal taste. But dogs frequently live up to their names, and so it is not a good idea to select one that is suggestive of high rank, for example Duke, Prince or Victor. Other names which may adversely influence matters include Buster, Tyson or Boxer. This is not to suggest that the dog knows the actual meanings of these names; the crucial point is that *you* know, and in using such a name you subconsciously bestow high rank upon your dog, a fact that will eventually become apparent to the dog.

In selecting a name, have several names in mind and try them out at moments when your puppy has its mind set firmly on some distraction. Settle for the name that most frequently triggers a positive response. After all, even though you may prefer a particular name, it is pointless if the dog ignores your choice; even worse, it may be the means by which you teach him to ignore your commands. If you have already made the wrong choice, change the name; rest assured, you can teach an old dog new tricks. Over the years, my own dogs have had names that I consider to be suggestive of a controllable character, or that are at least innocuous, such as Khaki, Harry, Kelly, Gentle, Angela and Sarah.

Castration and Spaying

The castration of male dogs and spaying of bitches accords with British Veterinary Association policy aimed at reducing the canine over-population within the United Kingdom. On a general basis the policy is for the common good, but on an individual basis it may or may not be wise. Make your choice, and if you decide on castration have it done when your puppy is at an age advised by your veterinarian.

Do not castrate adult dogs unless you have one that is over-sexed and turns his attention to inappropriate objects, or a cryptorchid (testicle failed to descend). Castration is wise for the former and essential for the latter condition, which represents a serious cancer risk (although this may change if at some time in the future successful treatment of such cancer becomes possible).

Bitches spayed before the age of three years often develop behavioural problems, in some cases antisocial aggression. However, a bitch can have as many as six or seven breeding seasons by the time she is three years old. Each unfertilized season represents an opportunity for infection of the uterus, when a veterinarian may quite rightly recommend spaying. Another problem is false pregnancy, which, if it occurs twice, necessitates spaying if the well-being of the bitch is to be the priority.

Diet and Bone Chemistry

Bone chemistry in relation to diet is a critical subject. When the calcium and phosphate intakes are out of balance orthopaedic problems may develop, especially in the joints or the tendons. Small terriers usually manifest tendon problems in the lower legs. Medium to large breeds present hip displasia or front shoulder maladies. Advice on these topics must necessarily be cautious, but the following text accords with my own experience and research.

During the maximum growth period of puppy development the importance of correct calcium and phosphate balance is essential, and dry meal, specially formulated for puppies by commercial animal feed manufacturers, is the surest and most convenient way of maintaining a balanced diet. Care must be taken to select the right preparation for the age of the puppy and to give the correct quantity. Feeding too much can be just as bad as feeding too little. Conditions such as hip dysplasia can result from poor diet, although this is by no means its only cause; others include trauma, too much or too little exercise, and, to a lesser extent, genetic susceptibility.

Heavy large-boned breeds may need vitamin C supplements, although the addition of supplements is usually unnecessary and may even be harmful. Owners should simply select the correct product variety for the age and energy requirement of their dog. If in doubt regarding a particular product's suitability, seek veterinary advice or consult the customer relations department of the manufacturer, which will welcome enquiries which may lead to more advanced research.

Orthopaedic Soundness

Much emphasis is placed on the use of X-rays to detect hip dysplasia. The procedure, however, is costly and, moreover, it is medically unethical to make an orthopaedic diagnosis on the strength of an X-ray. The X-ray should rather be used to confirm a diagnosis after clinical examination of the subject.

This particular malady was first diagnosed 330 years before the birth of Christ, and no one has been able to confirm the genetic link since that time, although there undeniably *is* a genetic influence. The name itself, dysplasia, is only a description, not a factual diagnosis, which might be rheumatoid, traumatic, infectious, osteo-arthritic or many other conditions.

Some dogs are pain insensitive and one could have quite severe joint problems which would be crippling to another dog, but which do not cause him any physical disability. Pain sensitivity could, of course, be a genetic influence. Specialist breeding presents a host of genetic influences, which is not surprising considering the extent to which primitive dog has been changed, from an animal about the size of a wolf with ears that pointed up to every unnatural size and shape imaginable, from the bulldog to the mastiff.

X-rays of a young puppy are of no value in determining what its eventual orthopaedic soundness will be. A dam and sire with sound hips do not always throw sound progeny. However, for some years puppies have been selected between seven and eight weeks of age for a wide variety of practical purposes through aptitude testing. The Brown Paper Test for bilateral limb soundness is of considerable value in determining the orthopaedic potential and practical worth of canine progeny.

To conduct the test, the puppy must first be 'stacked' (stood firmly four-square – as practised in the show ring) on a table with a highly polished surface. Stacking young puppies requires considerable patience and the procedure may take some time. Standard brown wrapping paper is placed under both rear feet, shiny side down. The tester carefully tries to rotate the paper clockwise and anticlockwise. Provided the puppy's rear legs are purchasing evenly downwards and both legs are uniform in length and of angular uniformity, the paper cannot be rotated unless considerable force is used. The test is repeated with an assistant gently pressing downwards on the puppy's rear. Normally the pup pushes back against the pressure and braces both rear legs uniformly. Similar procedures are carried out on the front legs and bilaterally on front and rear together.

Sound, physically well-balanced puppies at eight weeks of age, properly fed and exercised moderately to maturity, are not likely to suffer orthopaedic problems, other than by accidental injury.

Worming

All dogs suffer from parasitic worms. Regular worming is therefore essential, in accordance with veterinary advice for the geographic location in which you reside. Advice varies regarding the interval between dosage and the drugs used. Generally a puppy is wormed monthly from the age of four or five weeks until it is six months old, and thereafter every six months. Drug dosage also varies according to the weight of the puppy or dog.

Rest

Human beings need a regular six to eight hours of sleep every twenty-four hours, and dogs also require a regular ration of undisturbed rest. They require two hours per working day of total isolation. The definition of this isolation is peace and quiet with two closed doors between the dog and any other creature. Without this routine a dog, although he may appear to sleep, remains in a continuous state of semi-alertness. Such a state of affairs is not healthy or conducive to a long life. Deprived of regular isolation, nature takes over and every few days the dog will lapse into near stupor for several hours. Isolation also prevents the dog from becoming over-socialized with his owners.

Ceiling height is important to the dog when he is resting. Just as human beings are comfortable when their bedroom has a relatively low ceiling height of about 8ft (2.5m), so dogs enjoy just enough height and space to be able to stand up, turn around and lie at full stretch. The ideal piece of equipment as a dog bedroom and place of isolation is the modern folding kennel made from medium-gauge plated

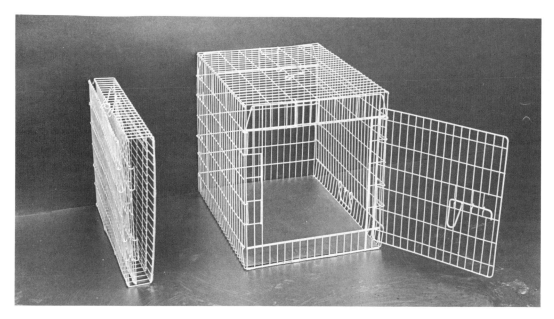

A portable, folding kennel is ideal for unsupervised control and safety. We humans may balk at what looks like caging but dogs do enjoy the security and privacy of these kennels. Do bear in mind, however, that no animal should be confined for more than a total of two hours during the working day. (Photo: Croft Engineering, Wigan).

wire. Novice dog owners may be shocked at the thought of caging a dog, ignoring the fact that their dog will enjoy the item as a comfortable den. The dog should sleep in this kennel, close to the family but at a lower level than human companions. When the dog fully adopts his kennel as a den the door need not be closed during the night hours, leaving him free to investigate incidents. If contained and isolated from the family, he will be unable to give immediate warning of fire or intruders.

There are many benefits of a daily two-hour isolation policy. It helps to balance a dog's dependence and independence of social contact with his owners, teaching him to enjoy his own company and never suffer from separation anxiety. As the kennel is portable, it is useful for dogs who get over-excited when visitors come to the home. Instead of shutting the dog away in the kitchen or utility room, which can cause an antisocial dislike of callers, he can be put in the kennel and still be able to see and learn from all that goes on. Visitors love to show that they are friendly to a resident dog, but their petting and fussing only reinforces canine excitement and undermines efforts to prevent jumping behaviour towards callers. The kennel protects the visitors from the dog and, more importantly, the dog from the visitors; both human and canine dignity are preserved.

The Dangerous Dogs Act

Knowledge of the 1991 Dangerous Dogs

Act is essential for all dog owners. Many people may think that this piece of legislation only applies to specific fighting breeds, but in fact the second section of the Act applies to all dogs and their owners. Since November 1991 an owner commits a serious criminal offence if his dog frightens a person and if the victim has reasonable cause to be frightened. The dog does not actually have to harm the person. If he does inflict harm, the offence is more serious. Harm covers more than aggression and biting; soiling or damaging clothing can be classed as harm. The usual punishment for a dog owner convicted under the Act is a heavy fine, but could also include a term of imprisonment. The punishment for the dog is usually execution. Losing control of him, therefore, could have fatal consequences for your best friend.

Even before this Act came into being, the law required dog owners to keep their dogs under proper control at all times. Sadly, only the minority of dog owners are able to conform to the old legislation, and the 1991 Act does little to encourage responsible dog ownership.

Recreation

It is very easy to forget your dog when he is in the garden unsupervised and what mischief he can get up to: fence-chasing neighbours and other dogs, digging the lawn, frightening tradesmen, and barking constantly. Some people believe that you should not own a dog unless you have a garden. Indeed, some breeders and rescue centres will not pass on a dog to flat dwellers. Whilst their policy seems sensible when measured by human standards, in practice the size of the home is irrelevant to the dog. Out of sheer necessity, a dog who inhabits a flat may have a greater number of outings than one who has access to a garden and he may therefore be the more socially well-balanced dog. Everything depends on the commitment of the individual owner.

Compulsion

How a dog is trained has considerable bearing on his well-being. Some trainers are excessive in their use of compulsion, even to the point of using force. Others describe techniques which avoid compulsion completely in the belief it is not necessary. Unfortunately, both human and canine worlds are far from perfect and a successful policy will take a middle course between these contrasting doctrines. Some degree of compulsion is required, but force and punishment are most unnecessary and easily become a barrier to the essential bond of trust and companionship between handler and dog.

Companionship

The family dog may love to meet and play with other dogs in the park, but prefers not to take playmates home. Many dog owners take on a second dog as company for the first. They believe, quite correctly, that their dog needs companionship, but this should come from the owner, not another dog.

Many households do accommodate a multi-dog family without problems, but this takes a great deal of patience and tolerance, as well as luck. Owning one dog is a heavy responsibility; adding a second more than doubles the obligation.

CHAPTER 6

Training Preparation

A good training programme will start with what might be called the *showing how* phase, followed by the *motivation* phase, when we make our dog want to please and respond correctly, by using reward in the form of sincere praise, the odd titbit or toys as objects of attraction. Using treats as a reward requires a degree of subtlety, defining the essential difference between bribery and reward.

Food has its place as an aid to learning; there is even a term for the procedure – variable reinforcement, by which a dog cannot be expected to get the treat every time. The technique transfers the mechanical procedure to the psychological, when the dog is denied a treat. For example: if when teaching the Recall you give your dog a titbit for the first three consecutive Recalls, then do a further three rewarding him with praise only, he will think 'Hey, what happened to my treat?' and will try progressively harder for the next two or three Recalls. Gradually he can be made to work harder and harder for each treat, until eventually the titbits become random. The dog is kept guessing, so he never knows when a refusal will cost him a treat. Consequently, it is not the giving which teaches him, but the absence of giving that imprints the required association in his mind. Over-reward the dog and he becomes bored and takes matters for granted, under-reward him and he will lose interest.

We can compare basic dog training exercises to building a pyramid. Each building block represents an individual basic exercise, while each new layer of blocks represents a training sequence and elevates control of canine response in small increments of distance and distraction. The cement which binds each block together consists of the ingredient FACE: Firmness, Accuracy, Compulsion and Encouragement.

Being *Firm* should not be an excuse for aggressive dominance on the part of the trainer; it is quite easy to be firm and retain a kindly attitude. *Accuracy* applies to the written or spoken word; student dog owners often hear but do not listen, and believe only what they want to believe from written text. Listening and seeing all is the key to accuracy in dog training practice. *Compulsion* is a subject which causes considerable controversy among dog training fraternities. Some believe it is possible to train a dog entirely on reward without any degree of compulsion; others advocate the severest of disciplinary measures. A middle course is best, using the minimum degree of compulsion necessary for the individual exercise, and in turn creating more opportunity for reward. *Encouragement* relates to reward, communicating handler pleasure to the dog when a dog responds correctly, in turn motivating him to enjoy purposeful learning.

Training Progress

Basic training should generally progress by weekly sequences. However, each owner must take into account personal idiosyncrasies as well as the quirks of his dog and set a pace for the training which fits in with individual circumstances, ability and time available. Progression from one sequence to another should never be in less than weekly increments, but, depending on time available and the commitment of the trainer, can take as long as a month. Changes of progressive pace and environmental circumstance will lead to setbacks not conducive to a dog reaching his full potential.

Assuming that trainers have time to match the proposed weekly pace of the programme, the timetable is broken down into two phases. First, the induction training – socializing the dog, establishing leadership and making him aware of the things he is *not* allowed to do – followed by eight weeks of basic training. Response to every command is compelled during the first three weeks of basic training, using handling technique and single verbal commands only, i.e: 'Sit', not 'Sit-Sit-Sit-Sit'. In week four the dog is allowed two or three seconds to respond correctly to each verbal command supported by a hand signal. Should he fail to respond correctly within a few seconds of a command being given, compulsion is applied without repeating the command or hand signal. Every correct response must be adequately rewarded with enthusiastic praise, *not* petting. Exceptions to this rule are after Play Recall and with sound-insensitive dogs, who must always be petted during the showing how training phase.

By the sixth week of an intensive training programme most dogs reach a learning plateau; the more a dog enjoys training, the greater will be the effect of this learning hiccup, which lasts about seven to ten days. During the fifth week the dog's responses to commands will have started to become automatic and he has time to think. Thinking allows confusion to enter the mental process, causing classic erroneous responses to commands. For example, when commanded 'Sit', the dog may respond with a posture which is half Sit and half Down and display either a mischievous or miserable facial expression. Handlers must discern the difference between their dog being confused, stressed or simply difficult. Confused dogs hampered by a learning plateau need to be reminded and shown again the correct response in a kind manner. This is best achieved by returning to the first sequence of the particular exercise and, in the same session, working through sequence by sequence to the current level of training.

Owners who have never previously trained a dog may, at first, find the theory complex. This need not be the case; most of the background knowledge is common sense and it will also help if the trainer understands how dogs think and how their minds work.

Human nature can cause problems in dog training. For example, although none of the basic exercises are difficult, an individual dog and trainer will find some easier or more useful than others. Their natural inclination will be to train more frequently on the successful exercises and almost ignore the least successful, when in fact the reverse should be the case. A practical balance must be maintained.

The exercises should also be balanced according to how highly strung and excitable the individual dog happens to be. Static exercises, such as Stays, flatten hyperexcitement. Practised in depth, Stay exercises have a short and long lasting effect: in the short term the dog Stays at the time of the command, and in the long term repeated Stays have the effect of calming excitable dogs. Consequently, the excitable hyperactive type of dog needs a high ratio of static to action exercises, and the timid reserved individual needs plenty of action.

Recreational walks, of course, count as action, and too often an owner of a hyperactive dog makes the mistake of thinking that a good run on open country or park land will take the steam out of their four-legged hooligan. When one hour does not have the desired effect, outings are either doubled in number or in duration. The effect of all this action on the dog is to increase his energy levels and to exacerbate excitement problems. Five minutes of training using the dog's brain has a much more calming effect than a five-mile run. Although daily walks are not a routine daily necessity, daily exercise is essential. It is possible, if not always wise, through using a little thought and planning to exercise a dog without getting out of your armchair.

Make sure you strike the right balance of action and static training with your dog and make allowances for the very young, or the older dog, who may be very set in its ways.

Commands

Learn the following vocabulary by heart until it becomes second nature. Doing so will avoid repetitive mistakes, such as commanding 'Oh come on', when you mean 'Dog's name, Heel' or 'Sit Down', when you mean either 'Sit' or 'Down'.

To Reward: 'OK', 'Good dog', 'Super dog' and 'Bravo'.
All must be given in a high-pitched tone of voice, motivating to the dog.

To Control: 'Sit', 'Down', 'Stand', 'Stay', 'Wait', 'Steady', 'Dog's name, Heel' and 'Dog's name, Come'.
Note that only the 'Come' and 'Heel' commands are preceded by the name of your dog. The purpose of this is to train your dog to work with anyone who knows his name but refuse to do so for strangers. For this reason, do not put your dog's name on the obligatory identity disc, use just your telephone number (including the area code). Control commands should be given with an authoritative tone of voice in accordance with the receptiveness of your dog.

To Admonish: 'Leave', 'Bad dog', 'That'll Do' and 'Enough'.
Remember that admonishments only interrupt a behaviour, they teach nothing. Your dog learns with the praise which follows admonishment, if and when he responds correctly. Admonishments should be given to prevent a sin, as an intervention. Corrections, in most instances, are too late.

Shouting at a dog when he is close is unnecessary. Admonishments should be growled at your dog, a complete contrast to rewarding verbal praise. Generally, lady trainers are too puny with admonishments to be effective, and men are too deep-voiced with praise.

Some dogs are absolutely flattened and deeply stressed by a harsh verbal command, while others, to pay any attention at all, seem to need a loud explosion to precede all commands. Each trainer must use a tone of voice conducive to the attentiveness of their dog, taking into account that a stressed dog will not learn anything useful.

Training Equipment

The dog leads sold at most pet shops come in a variety of useless sorts, such as the short chain lead with a trigger-hook at one end and a leather loop at the other, guaranteed to make your dog pull and give you blisters on your hands. Simplicity and versatility are the prime

A method of concertina folding a training lead to form a neat pad of material in the palm of the hand.

requirements for a dog training lead, which should be between 6ft and 7ft (1.8–2m), with a quality trigger-hook at one end and a loop with a metal ring

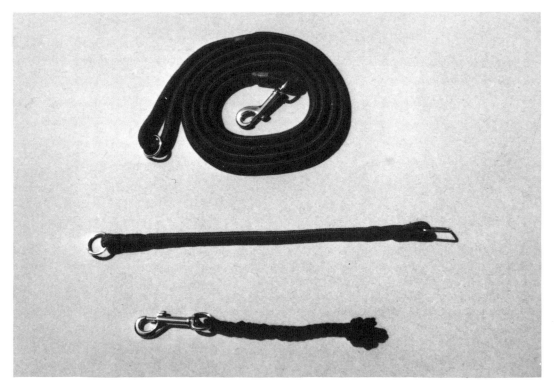

Essential training equipment. Top: the seven foot long training lead, with trigger hook and ring. Centre: training collar. Bottom: the tag lead.

at the other. When allowing a dog its head the lead can be used at full length. Formal Walking at Heel procedures require the lead to be halved, by placing the metal ring at the end loop in the trigger-hook attached to the dog collar. The lead should be made from a material kind to human hands, which can be easily folded into small loops and held firmly in the palm of the hand.

Dog training collars also come in a multitude of materials and patterns. Most common is the check-chain, which has a choke action. It is an excellent piece of equipment, provided it is used by a skilled handler, is of the correct size and has flattened links which do not pinch the dog's skin.

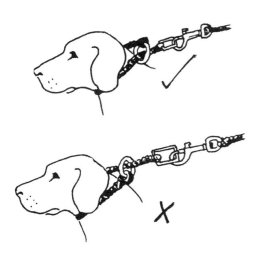

The right and wrong way to attach a training collar. A correct fit allows for two fingers to fit snugly under the back of the jaw, just behind the ears.

Novice owners will find two problems occur with check-chains. Firstly, the loop has to be made before placing it on the dog and passed over its head. Most dogs have a much larger head than neck, consequently the chain leaves several inches of surplus links which are unkind to human hands and can interfere with close control. Secondly, the chain, being loose, slips down against the dog's shoulders and encourages untrained canines to pull.

The illustrated rope collar is preferable for early sequences of dog training. It does not have to be pushed over the dog's head and fits tightly behind the ears and at the very front of the neck well clear of the choking reflex. It has a faster check action than a chain and is kind to long-haired dogs.

Tag leads, about 9in (23cm) in length, are useful for day-to-day handling of family dogs. Most dogs cannot resist chewing a tag lead when it is first attached to their collar. This chewing behaviour is ideal for teaching the command 'Leave', which momentarily interrupts the sin. Well-timed praise as the dog releases his grip on the tag lead teaches him, after a few repetitions, that he must not attack the article – with the qualification, in the presence of his owner. The lead should be removed at night and at other times when he is not under direct supervision. Once learned, the command 'Leave' can be used to interrupt any undesirable behaviour at a given moment.

A tag lead for handling around the house and teaching the 'Leave' command.

An everyday collar complete with statutory identity disk.

Another benefit of this useful piece of equipment is that owners learn to keep their hands low when handling their dog. It also guards against over-handling; hands should be instruments of affection, not affliction. Mouthing of hands with needle-sharp puppy teeth is also avoided with proper use of a tag lead.

PART 2
BASIC TRAINING

CHAPTER 7

Lesson 1: Induction

Early Days

Prior to the arrival of a new dog or puppy, decisions need to be made regarding its sleeping arrangements, feeding, socializing, veterinary requirements especially vaccinations and worming, health and third party insurance, physical exercise, and arrangements for family holidays – good boarding kennels are usually booked a year ahead for school holiday periods.

Ground rules should also be decided in advance, with a firm resolve being made not to spoil the dog: no titbits between meals (except when training); he will not be treated by adult or child as a teddy bear; love will not be shown until he is controllable and deserving of affection; he will be made to learn his place in the family rank, and will become a credit to the family and community.

House-training

Training a dog to be clean in the house covers a wide spectrum of circumstances: the young puppy between seven and eight weeks of age, adult rescue dogs and infirm senile veterans. Provided the trainer has the time and commitment, house-training is one of the easiest things to teach any fit healthy dog.

House-Training a Puppy

Puppies spend a great deal of time each day sleeping and resting. This may surprise some owners who are more aware of the intensive daily periods of high activity their particular puppy displays.

Puppies and dogs tend to use the same general area each time they excrete. Consequently, when arriving home with your new family member it is a mistake to take him straight indoors. Regardless of the weather, take the pup to a pre-selected area of the garden which you have planned to be the canine latrine. Supervise puppy exploratory behaviour and at the moment it starts to urinate or excrete, give the command 'Do Business'. Make sure you transmit with plenty of praise how pleased you are that the first excretion or urination has been outdoors.

Take your puppy indoors to the kitchen or utility room and for the time being restrict him to that area of the house. Pups urinate within a few moments of waking up, and open their bowels within fifteen minutes of being fed and on other odd occasions. Use this knowledge to anticipate the need to get him swiftly outdoors to the latrine area. Repeat the 'Do Business' command several times. When young puppies intend to open their bowels, they usually spend several seconds circling backwards in a semi-crouched position, a clear warning to the observant owner that things are about to happen and that the puppy needs to be quickly taken outside.

Allow for indoor accidents by placing newspaper down over a large area adjacent to the exit door of the pup's nursery area. Under no circumstances allow the pup access to carpeted areas of the house until it is house-trained, which should take a maximum of seven days. Most puppies find newspaper an excellent material on which to deposit their waste body products. Over a few days gradually reduce the area of newspaper and move it closer to the door. Eventually place the paper under the closed door with just about an inch of it on the inside. The pup will want to excrete on the paper but as there is not enough it will scratch at the paper, trying to pull it from under the door. Interpret this as asking to go out. After a few repetitions of taking the pup outdoors when it scratches the paper you can dispense with paper altogether; your pup will have learned to ask to be let out, although only during the working day.

Night-Time Control

During the night hours your puppy or dog should be confined in a small area. A 3ft by 3ft (92cm by 92cm) puppy pen or an indoor folding kennel, properly fitted out with suitable bedding (not straw) and a calf's hoof to chew, make ideal sleeping quarters. Puppies and dogs will not soil their own bed space, unless they are ill or confined too long, but will try to withhold until they are released in the morning. Do not feed after 8pm and take the water bowl away at 8.15pm. Many canine textbooks advocate leaving water down all the time, but doing so is not hygienic, a bowl of water after it has been down for

fifteen minutes is filthy. Water must be boiled until the puppy is three months old, so stock up each day with cooled boiled water.

Dogs have their own internal alarm clocks; the first signs of daylight trigger ablution time and action. They also have another associated signal, the dawn bird chorus, which you probably sleep through unaware of the cacophony birds make. Measures need to be taken to keep your dog sleeping until you arise. Windows should be shielded, a task which is easier said than done. However, if an indoor kennel is used it is a simple matter to blank out daylight with a cloth cover without inhibiting ventilation. Background sound from a radio also helps. Make putting your puppy outdoors your first priority on rising.

Exceptions to the Rule

Modern agricultural policy has encouraged farmers to diversify into non-food production, and one area which has been actively encouraged by government bureaucrats is the setting-up of intensive puppy breeding units. Some breeds can fetch a high price. Although grants are not available directly for puppy breeding, money is given for every acre of agricultural land taken out of use and a few litters of puppies can more than replace the revenue expected from a considerable acreage of redundant land.

Intensive puppy farming methods have brought about a profusion of 'binned pups', so-called because from day one they are reared in upright plastic dustbins and do not even get a glimpse of the outside world until the day they are sold, usually to a dealer at six weeks of age or younger. Such puppies have become used to living in their own excreta, are neurotic and wet themselves at the slightest strange sound or movement.

Farmers needing to diversify are not the only culprits, some established breeders cashing in on show dog glory are almost as bad, rearing too many pups in too small a space and with too little tender loving care. The Kennel Club has introduced measures to restrict the number of litters that can be registered, and has gone to a great deal of expense to computerize and speed up its registration procedures, so there is now no excuse for a breeder not to have the KC Registration Document on the day of sale. These measures do not greatly impair puppy farmers, but they make it easier for people to identify a risky purchase.

Binned pups are a fact of life in today's society; numerous and pitiful creatures. Buyers do beware, make sure you go to a recommended and reputable caring breeder, see the dam, and have the Kennel Club Registration Document with a bill of sale in your hand before parting with your money. Also, have the puppy checked over by your veterinarian within the first forty-eight hours after collection.

Other exceptions to the rule include sick puppies. Messing the den can be the first sign of illness and the need to consult your veterinarian. Sick puppies can dehydrate very quickly, so you must be observant and take stock of your individual pup's normal water intake and output habits; any deviation from the norm is a sign that an illness may be incubating and water must then be available at all times.

The final exception to the rule is, of course, the dog who messes through being confined for too long a period.

Prolific Soiling

Owners who are unfortunate enough to have a puppy or dog who despite all precautions repeatedly soils indoors, and even in some cases comes indoors to do his business, need to keep biological time-charts for urination, bowel motions and feeding times. After a few days the charts will show a pattern through which the times the dog needs to be outdoors can easily be anticipated. Your dog can be put outdoors at likely times until you are certain he has 'performed' (observation and supervision are necessary).

Elderly Infirm Dogs

Indoor accidents are not uncommon with elderly dogs once they become infirm. Bitches, especially, can develop leaky bladders and release the odd few drops of urine about the house during the day and large puddles at night. Bitch urine smells offensive at the best of times, but the older they become, the worse the stench. The accidents usually occur in the aged dog's favourite resting-place in the house, perhaps in front of the hearth or under the kitchen table.

The incontinent bitch, although a very restful dog, does have moments of high activity and apart from old age is not necessarily a sick dog. Surgery can be an option to tighten the sphincter muscle, but anaesthesia in an elderly dog is not without risk and is best avoided unless absolutely essential.

Treat the elderly dog like a puppy: the moment he wakes up, out he goes until he has emptied his bowels. Lay newspaper down on favourite rest areas and place a synthetic sheepskin on top of the paper. The skin is easy to wash, the paper can be burned and any urinary leaks which occur while the dog is sleeping will not permanently taint the household atmosphere.

Cleaning Up Accidents

Clean up accidents with soap and water and disinfectant. Pine disinfectant has an aroma which will encourage a dog to use the same location again. So, having cleaned up with disinfectant, go over the area with a very dilute solution of cider vinegar, not strong enough to be detected by your own nostrils. Dogs, who have much more sensitive noses, do not generally like this scent, and often have a strong dislike of it. When dry, spray the room with your normal household aerosol.

This method works by association. Attracted by the aroma of pine, your dog soils the scented area and the residual combination of pine and previous urine or excreta triggers him to use the same location on other occasions. The cider vinegar, however, discourages further accidents and his dislike is associated with the smell of the household aerosol, which, in common use throughout the home, acts as a lasting deterrent to indoor fouling. There are a few exceptions, and some dogs will actually drink cider vinegar. Hopefully though, this tip will help most dog owners when house-training their dogs.

Stud Dog Dominance

Naïve pet dog owners often think it a good idea to let Bess and Rover get together to satisfy an imagined need for passion, or perhaps a mating takes place by accident without the owners' knowledge. Once a dog has experience as a sire, he thinks he is king of the universe and announces this promotion on the canine social ladder by cocking his leg over everything: door jams, family beds, your underwear, even the family cat, and, for sure, when you are dressed up for a night out he will not miss the opportunity to scent-post your finery just as you are about to step out the front door. He wants the Toast Master and all the guests at your intended function to know that he is at home and available. One experience is enough for the trait to become a lifelong habit and the amount of time needed to counter-condition the problem is impractical for most domestic situations.

The best remedy is prevention. Keep your dog away from bitches in season and forget the idea of giving him a mate. Dogs with a normal sex drive who have had no reproductive experience usually start to become less interested in copulation between the ages of three and four years.

Castration

Castration is an excellent means of preventing dogs from laying urinary scent-posts. However, it should be done when they are still puppies after the age of six months, at a time recommended by your veterinarian. Other than for sexual aggression or for prophylactic risk of secondary diseases (risk of cancer), do not have an adult dog castrated, as in my experience this can cause aggression.

Some castrated dogs continue to cock their legs and lay down scent-posts, but this is rarely the case when the operation is carried out during pre-adolescence.

Effects of Diet

Changes in diet are not easily tolerated

by the canine digestive system and it can take up to three days or more for a dog to adjust to a new diet. Motions easily become loose during the change-over and accidental bowel movements become a possibility.

Some dog owners go on feeding their dog the same diet year after year and take no account that an elderly dog needs to be fed a diet less rich than during his prime of life. Diets which are too rich for the dog can cause scouring, so do not be too quick to accept that an old dog who is not clean overnight has a problem you must live with.

Punishment

Elimination of body waste is a natural function and it is pure stupidity to admonish or punish a dog for messing indoors. Many who imagine themselves to be experts advocate rubbing a dog's nose in it when he messes indoors, claiming this will cure him. The object, however, is not to stop a dog messing, but to train him not to do so indoors.

Dogs are great lateral thinkers and if a dog is punished for messing he would be stupid to mess again in the presence of his owner. Taken out last thing at night, for ten minutes or forty minutes, he does not eliminate. Back home, he is put away for the night in the kitchen. His owner comes down in the morning and there is no mess, everything is spotless. Several days pass and the kitchen is clean each morning. His owner is pleased and thinks punishment has been effective until one night, a few minutes after putting his dog to bed, the owner, having forgotten something, returns to the kitchen and steps straight into a pile of dog muck. What happened? When punished the dog learned that it is not a good idea to excrete in the presence of his owner. He had continued messing in the kitchen at night, but to avoid punishment had been eating his own excreta. When the owner entered the room before he had the opportunity to complete his own waste disposal act, he knew the presence of his owner and the muck were bad news, and cowered in the corner to distance himself from the anger and shock of his owner. He could not understand why the natural function of opening his bowels was wrong.

Dog Mess Disposal

Without doubt, dogs produce a profuse amount of mess which responsible dog owners should dispose of without delay. Excreta in the garden should be picked up and flushed down the toilet, the sooner after the event the better.

When outdoors in public places with your dog, always carry a plastic freezer bag; if your dog messes, don the bag like a glove, pick up the excrement, turn the bag outside in, tie a knot in it to seal the contents and, as soon as possible, discard in the nearest waste bin. Some people do not wish to learn this aspect of responsible dog ownership, and can be seen every day in the streets, looking up at the sky while their dog excretes and pretending it is not happening. Not only do the anti-dog brigade hate such people, the responsible dog owning fraternity despise them even more.

Toxocara Canis

The poor dog alone is blamed for conveying *Toxocara* (canine roundworm) to humans, especially children. No one seems to question why some children go blind through this malady and others do not become afflicted. The answer lies in pollution and how it can undermine the human immune system. Normal healthy human beings have a very high degree of immunity to canine roundworms. A contributory factor to the incidence of *Toxocara* is the lack of soil control procedures by local authorities who should test regularly for the levels of *Toxocara* and other pollutants in public parks. This used to be a standard procedure during the days of Public Health Inspectors, but is not so now in many Environmental Health Authorities.

Dogs do need regular worming with a proprietary oral drug recommended by your veterinarian. Puppies should be wormed monthly after leaving the breeder until six months old, thereafter every six months. No dog, however clean, is immune to worms.

Always pick up your dog's excreta.

Eliminate on Command

Owners who teach their dogs to eliminate on command rarely have to use a plastic bag in public places. Some dogs will only excrete in their own gardens, which is not a bad thing, and suffer agony if taken out for a whole day. Regular use of the command 'Do Business', followed by praise and perhaps a titbit each time you see your dog excrete, will in less than a few days imprint the required response wherever you are at the time. Consistent repetitions produce a sure automatic reaction to the command, as easily, if not more so, than with the Auto Sit exercise. Training a dog to eliminate on command is much easier and less time-consuming than teaching a human baby to use a potty.

Lead Training a Puppy

The term puppy covers a wide age group, up to twelve months, and an even wider range of physical size. Consequently, common sense must be applied to match the following advice to the size and maturity of your puppy.

Very young pups can be taught walking at heel without a lead. First they must learn to follow you. This is easily achieved at meal-times by walking backwards away from the puppy and at the same time calling it by name. Once the message to follow you closely when you walk backwards with the feeding bowl becomes firmly implanted in the puppy's mind, distance can be increased, and you can turn round and continue for a few paces in the same direction as the puppy. The command 'Puppy's Name, Heel' can be given in a motivating tone of voice when turning round.

The next step is to attach a lead for the puppy to tow loosely behind it. When the pup becomes used to the attachment, the above procedures can be repeated on several occasions each day.

The illustrations overleaf show a puppy being taught to Walk at Heel on Lead using titbits instead of a feeding bowl. When walking at heel learning has been firmly imprinted with a happy association, you can almost dispense with the titbits.

Over-Handling

Teaching inexperienced dog handlers the correct attitude towards controlling a dog on lead is not the easiest of instructional tasks. Everything is fine, until the person places his hands on the lead. The problem

Teaching a puppy to Follow by walking backwards, using a titbit as an incentive. Once the puppy is happy closely following the handler, it is a simple matter to Pirouette Right and Walk on with the handler and puppy heading in the same direction. This illustration shows the handler ready to negotiate the change to Walk at Heel.

Here the handler has just completed the Right About Turn and using plenty of verbal encouragement, the two Walk on happily.

is that novice handlers are inclined to approach each basic exercise as if they were reading a step-by-step manual. Unfortunately, the dog's first impression at the receiving end of this is along the lines of 'This idiot does not know what he is doing'. Consequently, the situation should be one in which the handler is performing everyday tasks, at which he is fully competent, and is able to control his dog using a hands-off technique, for

which the following lead around waist method is ideal.

For two hours each day (although not necessarily a single two-hour period) the lead is placed behind the handler's waist, loop to the left, trigger-hook to the right. The trigger-hook is taken round the front, threaded through the loop and pulled tight, leaving the loop by the handler's left hip and the trigger-hook free for attaching to the dog's collar. The lead now acts as an umbilical cord of communication, handler to dog. Disregarding the dog, the handler then proceeds about daily household tasks, washing-up, gardening, watching television, or whatever.

'Look Mum, no hands!' Teaching a West Highland White Terrier puppy to follow using the no hands wrap around waist technique. The handler must have a very positive attitude and use common sense. If the dog stops, or is distracted, the handler must continue walking, at a kindly pace, in the intended direction. Tangling of the lead is avoided by the handler circling left or right.
Note: *The dog should be kept on the left hand side of the handler.*

While doing so the dog, kept at the left side, is ignored, and hand contact with the lead is kept to an absolute minimum.

Several messages are transmitted down the lead to the dog as the handler performs everyday tasks, including follow or lose your head, what a pack leader, pay attention and concentrate. The technique must be applied with common sense. Whether at the kitchen sink, gardening, washing the car, or reading, the dog must follow his handler and, in kindly manner, learns that he is the junior partner in the relationship. The dog responds to being ignored and being made to feel unwanted by becoming extremely attentive.

Socializing

Puppies and dogs must be shown what behaviour is expected of them in a variety of situations. Unfortunately pups should not be subjected to long walks until they are between ten and twelve months old, depending on whether they are a small or large breed. Until then their bones are not sufficiently hardened to endure prolonged exercise. This does not mean, however, that they cannot be out for many hours each day, provided a policy of walk for ten minutes, rest for fifteen is followed and two or three breaks are taken to allow the pup to have a well-deserved nap. Older dogs also benefit from this socializing policy, as it allows new experiences to be introduced gradually.

Ideally, when taking charge of a new puppy or dog you should have two or three weeks free from most other responsibilities, allowing you sufficient time to introduce the pupil to the postman, milkman and other callers or visitors, to show that they are friendly and part of the normal day-to-day events at home and in the community. Outings should include plenty of street walking, as well as regular visits to the local shopping precinct, riding stables (with the consent of the owners), schools, bridle-paths, carparks, and common land. Marked vocal contrast between praise and admonishments shows the student dog what behaviour is acceptable and what is not.

Preliminary Training

From day one the primary objective must be control. This requires a great deal of direct supervision, without which a new canine arrival runs the risk of rapidly becoming a hooligan. The basic training procedures of Sit, Stand, Down, Stay and Come are referred to as control exercises.

Sit-Stand-Down

This is a block exercise which should be trained twice a day using fifteen changes of position on each occasion. Problems of anticipation can arise; for example if the same sequence of commands is always used, 'Sit', 'Stand' and 'Down', when the Sit-Stay exercise is performed the dog may anticipate that 'Stand' will come next and in an effort to please and show

how smart he is, break the Stay by coming to the Stand position. Consequently, some small variety in the rotation of commands is essential.

Do not try to place your dog in the Down position from a Stand during this induction phase. When teaching this exercise you must be certain your dog is learning what you intend and not something completely alien to your purpose.

One common training error is to use uniform time intervals between commands. For example, if you silently count to yourself 'one and two and' up to five seconds between each command, you are training your dog to move every five seconds. Hence, the interval between commands must be varied between a couple of seconds and half a minute. During early sequences of this exercise the dog is held in position for the required interval.

Do not pet your dog during this exercise, instead talk to him in a reassuring manner.

Stand

With the dog in the Sit position, kneel on the floor, facing his right side, with his head to your right. Place two fingers of your right hand in the training collar and clench your fist, holding him firmly at the side of the face and just behind his right ear. This hold prevents your dog from mouthing your hands.

Place your left hand, palm down, beneath the dog's abdomen. Apply forward pressure with your right hand. With your left hand (or arm with medium and large dogs) apply pressure against the front of the hind legs, while at the same time giving the command 'St-a-a-a-a-nd'. Accentuate clearly the 'a-n-d' in a singing treble tone of voice. Praise and reassure.

Preparing to Stand. The right hand should be placed in the collar from front to rear behind the dog's right ear. The left hand and part of the forearm must be positioned beneath the abdomen, against the front of the dog's hind legs. The hands are then stretched apart as if opening an accordion, whilst giving the command 'St-a-a-a-a-nd' as the dog responds, and finally 'Super dog, well done'.

Keep the dog's head up and spine straight. Do not apply pressure under the dog's abdomen, as this will cause him to roach his lumber spine. If your left hand or arm is too low the dog will step over it; if it is too high you will force him to assume a roached-backed stance, which with many repetitions may damage his spine.

The completed Stand with the dog held 'stacked' in a good posture. The front legs are straight like two parallel gun barrels, with the rear hocks at right angles to the ground.

Sit using the tuck over tail method. The handler does not exert pressure against the dog's spine or hips, and opts instead for a gentle hand movement with a see-saw action (right hand upwards, left hand downwards). The right hand then strokes from behind the dog's ears, down the spine and over the tail.

The completed Sit from Stand position showing the correct right hand position on the collar. Two fingers are inserted in the collar and the fist clenched behind the dog's ears to prevent mouthing.

Sit

Kneel with your dog as in the Stand exercise. Again, place two fingers of your right hand in the training collar and clench your fist, holding the dog firmly at the side of his face and just behind his right ear. With your left hand stroke from behind the dog's ears, down his back, tuck over the tail then bring your left hand forwards behind the dog's knees, compelling him to sit, at the same time commanding 'Sit'.

Down

Continue kneeling and retain your hold on the training collar with your right hand. Place your left arm over the dog's shoulders (withers) and lift the leg furthest from you, at the same time applying pressure with your upper left arm against the dog's withers. This prevents the dog from standing up. Do not grip his leg with your thumb or use a scissor grip with your

Placing the dog Down from the Sit position. One at a time, beginning with the leg furthest from the handler, the front legs are raised by hand pressure from behind until the dog assumes a near begging position. During a pause, the dog is reassured verbally, then with forearm pressure over the withers, is lowered into the Down position. The front legs are the last part of the anatomy to make contact with the ground.

Note: Use a single Down command as the dog is being lowered. Do not grip the legs.

The Down nearly completed; all that remains is for the handler to slide the hands out from under the dog's legs. Note once again that the legs are not actually gripped.

An alternative method for the Down which is more suited to large breeds.

fingers. Try to avoid touching his leg joints; lift between the joints, as most dogs are touch sensitive on their leg joints.

Lift the near-side leg using your right hand and bring the dog into a begging posture. Pause, praise and reassure the dog, at the same time balancing your own posture ready for the next move.

Using pressure with your left arm against the dog's withers, gently compel him down. The dog's front legs are the last part of his anatomy to make contact with the ground. Command 'Down' as you do so. Praise and reassure.

Sit from Down

Place two fingers of your left hand in the collar, from behind to front at a point between his ears. Place your right hand between his front legs against his chest (not throat). Pull and lift the dog into Sit position with his front legs just clearing the floor. Drop the dog's front legs to the floor, at the same time giving the single command 'Sit'.

Sit from Down. Two fingers of the left hand are placed in the collar between the ears, from rear to front, with the right hand on the chest between the front legs. The dog is lifted until the front legs just clear ground level, then as the feet are dropped the Sit command is given.

After each command and change of position, praise and reassure but do not pet the dog. Keep his head up and tail wagging in response to your commands. Train twice each day, with fifteen changes of position as a block exercise. Stand no nonsense; if your dog plays up, give a short sharp shake at the side of his neck against the training collar with your right hand and growl 'Bad dog', following up with praise and reassurance.

Walking at Heel

Very young puppies should be introduced to a collar first, preferably a non-choke flat cloth or round leather type, fitted tightly enough to allow only two fingers to be inserted comfortably between the collar and neck. Tightness and wear should be checked on a daily basis as young pups grow quickly. The collar that is a perfect fit one day may not be so the next. Your puppy may at first claw furiously at the collar, displaying considerable *mock* distress. Do not worry, after a few minutes it will get used to the idea and allow other distractions to occupy its mind.

Next, with either puppy or adult dog, a tag lead of between 6in and 11in (15–27cm), depending on the size of the dog, is attached to the D-ring of the collar and allowed to hang down below the dog's chin. This serves two purposes: being able to control a puppy in a manner which avoids needle-sharp teeth, and teaching the command 'Leave' as a verbal admonishment to interrupt undesirable behaviour at any given moment. Normally the puppy cannot resist chewing the tag lead; when it does so, the command 'Leave' is given in a strong low-pitched tone of voice, sufficiently intense to shock.

Immediately the puppy releases the item, it is praised reassuringly in a rewarding tone of voice. The procedure may have to be repeated a few times before the lesson is learned. Remember that admonishments only interrupt the behaviour and teach nothing. Learning only takes place as a result of the vocal praise which follows admonishment, when the dog responds correctly.

The tag lead must be removed when the dog is unattended.

Teaching a Mature Dog to Follow

Place a 7ft (2m) lead around your waist, with the loop of the lead by your left hip. Bring the lead from behind you, round your waist and thread it through the loop, pull it tight and attach it to the collar on your dog. Then, in a positive manner, go about your day-to-day business, ignoring, to the best of your ability, your attached companion and trying to keep him at or near your left side. Do not touch the lead. The first five minutes may be a little problematic, but persevere.

This places you in the position of being pack leader, performing tasks when you know what you are doing, and at the same time controlling your dog with the minimum of effort. Should your dog stubbornly resist, do not tow him around as if he were a brick behind you. Use common sense and motivate him in a happy tone of voice. You have to convey the message that following you is fun. Do not be unkind physically, but if the dog shows a fear response do not try to reassure him verbally, doing so will reward what is in his mind at the given moment – fear. Instead, continue what you are doing in a matter-of-fact attitude and be prepared for the moment your dog attempts to overcome his fear. When he does so, give him a verbal reward. Use patience and common sense, not force.

Practise this procedure for a total of two hours each working day. After four or five days progress to the next sequence, Auto Sit and False Start (*see* Chapter 8).

Long Down Sequence 1

This exercise is the foundation stone of the whole training syllabus as it relates to how your dog identifies dominance and intelligence. Dogs instinctively respect creatures who are faster and stronger at close-quarters and in turn credit them with being more intelligent. Once you achieve this status in the mind of your dog, he will attempt to gain your favour. Treat the exercise as a game, which you must always win, and you will discover the art of making your dog want to please.

The exercise lasts for thirty minutes. Success is not measured by how long your dog stays down without attempting to move. Quite the reverse is true: the more he tries to move and the more often you prevent him from doing so, the greater your achievement.

The Long Down. This Bernese Mountain Dog is alerted by distractions and about to break from the Down, but is prevented from doing so by the handler pressing on the shoulders and repeating the Down command.

Complete five thirty-minute Long Down exercises during the next week, but do not do two on the same day. There must be no distraction until induction is over and you start week one (Lesson 2) of the basic syllabus.

Entry-Exit Discipline

This is another dominance exercise. On-lead or off-lead, indoors or out, never allow your dog to advance through an opening in front of you.

Begin on-lead in the Control position (Sit at heel) and advance with your dog to the door or gate. At the threshold, slacken the lead and command the dog firmly 'Wait'. If necessary, snap-check the dog to a position immediately behind and to your left.

Step through the door with your right foot first. Halt, pause, praise the dog if he waits. Prevent him from moving before commanded to do so with further snap-checks on the lead and a sharp verbal 'Ah!' After you have checked it is safe to proceed, command your dog 'Dog's name, Heel', and walk on.

After a few paces, turn and repeat the procedure in the opposite direction.

Complete six consecutive entrances and exits twice a day. Do not always use the same location.

The exception to the Entry-Exit discipline concerns public buildings and transport with automatic doors, when handler and dog must enter together in close contact.

Normally for Entry-Exit discipline the dog is made to Wait whilst the handler goes first, but automatic doors require dog and handler to proceed together in unison.

Disaster may strike if automatic door Entry-Exit discipline is not executed properly.

CHAPTER 8

Lesson 2

Introduction

Early training should continue through-out each day, taking one or two minutes here and there as the opportunity arises. Between these times try to ignore your dog, making him feel unwanted, but do be sincere and generous with reassurance and praise when you are training and learning together. The contrast between being ignored and receiving attention will give your dog a pleasant association with training, and will make him want to please you.

Give commands to your dog once only, then compel the correct response in as gentle a manner as possible. Praise each correct response sincerely. Make every effort to ensure your dog enjoys being trained and do not expect too much too soon.

Distance Control Sequence 1

Sit

Attach the training collar and tag lead to your dog, place him in the Stand position and kneel on the floor facing him. With your left hand bring the tag lead to a central point immediately above the dog's ears. Have a titbit in your right hand, palm towards the dog's face. Gently pull

straight upwards on the tag lead with your left hand, and at the same time raise your right hand to a point just over and behind the head of your dog.

As he starts to adopt the Sit position, give the verbal 'Sit' command and praise reassuringly. The timing of the command is important; it must be given with a firm voice at the exact instant your dog starts to adopt the Sit position and praise must follow while he is still thinking 'Sit'.

The Sit. The handler compels the dog into the Sit from the Down position. A titbit in the right hand is held with the palm towards the dog and travels in an upward arc to a point just above the snout as the dog comes into the correct Sit posture.

Reward with the titbit the instant dog sits. One fraction of a second late or premature with the titbit, and the reward will not be associated with 'Sit'.

Down

Commence with the dog in the Stand or Sit position. Have a third treat in your right hand. Hold the tag lead beneath the dog's chin with your left hand, and apply pressure downwards and toward the dog's tail with your straight left arm. At the same time move your right arm and hand in an L-shape from above your right shoulder to ground level and then towards your body, with your palm upwards, exposing the treat to your dog.

The only way he can get the treat, if you maintain the direction of your left-hand pressure, is by going down. The first time you do this allow several seconds for your dog to work out the body mechanics of reaching the titbit. Rewards of praise and reassurance are as for the other positions.

> *General note: Although the frequency of titbit rewards should be gradually reduced once the association becomes fixed in the dog's mind, sincere praise must continue for every correct response. Remember, commands should be given only once. If commands are repeated the dog is detrained rather than trained.*

The Down. With the dog in the correct Sit position, the handler's extended right arm travels in a downward arc, coming to rest just in front of the dog's feet.

The completed Down. Having moved the reward through three positions, with varied time intervals between commands, the dog is allowed the titbit. Over the next few days, each treat should gradually become more difficult to earn.

The Stand. From the Sit or Down position, the dog is commanded with a high-pitched, motivating voice 'St-a-a-a-a-nd'. At the same time, a titbit held in the right hand is placed against the snout and is then directed towards the handler, the hand parallel with the floor.

Stand

Continue kneeling face-to-face with your dog. Hold the tag lead beneath his chin with your right hand which contains a second treat. As the dog starts to adopt the stand position, give the command 'St-a-a-a-a-nd' then praise and reassure. Reward with the second titbit the instant the dog adopts the position. Prevent him from coming too far forward with pressure from your right hand against his chest.

HOMEWORK

Twice each day practise two blocks of distance control exercises, with fifteen changes of position on each occasion. On the first day be generous with titbit rewards, but gradually make your dog work harder and harder for each treat.

Formal Walking at Heel Sequence 1

Train your dog twice each day with the following simple exercises. Heel training periods should never be less than two or more than five minutes in duration. The procedures must be treated as a game by using plenty of verbal encouragement, and you must be very generous with your praise.

Previously, when using the hands-off technique with the lead around your

The Control position. The lead should be held in the right hand only, travelling across the handler's thigh, above the knee, with about two inches of slack between handler and dog. Both should face in exactly the same direction, with the dog's front legs in line with the handler's legs.

The Halt. Each time the handler halts, the left hand must grip the lead close to the collar and manipulate the dog into a close at heel position. The handler should then change hands to compel Sit with the tuck over tail method.

The Auto Sit. With the left hand, the handler strokes from behind the ears, down the spine, to tuck over the tail. The right hand maintains tension on the lead, which comes upwards at a right angle to a central point between the dog's ears. Praise must be enthusiastic and should commence as the dog begins to move into the Sit position.
Note*: No command is given, as the training will eventually condition an automatic response each time the handler halts. To achieve this, it is necessary to complete six consecutive Auto Sits twice a day.*

waist, your dog had to follow you. Now, with your hands on the lead, the classic handler sin of following the dog may creep in – *if* you allow it to.

Auto Sit

Begin in the on-lead Control position with your dog sitting properly at Heel at your left side, and with just 2–3in (5–7cm) of slack lead between you.

Step one pace forward with your left foot, as you do so give the command 'Dog's name'. Without hesitation take another step with your right foot and command 'Heel'. Halt by locking your left foot to your right, and at the same time take hold of your dog's collar with your left

hand. Change hands left to right and sit your dog using the tuck-over-tail method. Stand up straight and praise your dog sincerely.

Do not give a command as you sit your dog. The goal is to teach your dog to sit automatically every time you halt when Walking at Heel together. The response is ideal as a kerb drill at road crossings and when you stop to talk in the street.

HOMEWORK

Twice each day train six consecutive Auto Sits in quick succession. Use plenty of motivating praise and expressive body language. There is a four-count rhythm to the exercise: 'Dog's name, Heel', change hands, dog sitting at heel. Silently count to yourself, one, two, three, four. Use a slow tempo until you both become used to the procedure and build up a fast rhythm gradually as the week progresses.

After the sixth Auto Sit, immediately follow on with the next exercise.

TIPS

The Auto Sit and False Start exercises can, for the handler, be a little back-breaking. You can avoid this to some extent if you bend from your knees, instead of bending down and over the dog. Handlers with very small dogs may need to kneel down quickly on their right knee to sit their dog using the tuck-in method.

Make sure you are not slovenly in your handling and do not push down on the dog's hind-quarter, as this, through repetition, will damage the hip joints and perhaps even displace a spinal disc. When holding the collar do not twist your fingers or wrist, as doing so turns the collar into a tourniquet, and your dog will not sit when you throttle him.

The False Start. From the Sit at Heel position, the handler advances right foot first, two paces ahead of the dog. This illustration shows the pause prior to commanding 'Dog's name, Heel'. By changing the lead from the left to the right hand, the dog is compelled into the Sit at Heel position as for the Auto Sit.

False Start

This exercise requires the handler to advance two paces in a straight line ahead of the dog, who must remain sitting in an attentive manner. No command is given as the handler leaves the dog. Do not jerk the lead as you advance; if you do so, you signal your dog to move.

Without command step forward two paces, right foot first, and halt by locking right foot to left. Pause for several seconds with your back towards your dog then, using the command 'Dog's name, Heel', bring your dog to the Sit at Heel position using the tuck-in method.

General note: Mixing Auto Sit and False Start exercises teaches a dog to be attentive. Remember to advance left foot first for the Auto Sit and right foot first for the False Start.

Pay Attention Sequence 1

Training a dog to be attentive during formal Walking at Heel exercises relies on techniques to keep him guessing as to where your next footfall will be. Primarily this requires plenty of verbal encouragement, sufficiently stimulating that it is impossible for the dog to ignore the handler. Add to this a very positive handler stride at a suitable pace on a short but slack lead, and the stage is set for the guessing game.

Following the consecutive Auto Sit and False Start training, a short session of mixing the two exercises together compels the dog to pay attention.

Pay Attention. Enticing objects help to retain and/or trigger the dog's attention back to the handler. Titbits and soft toys generally do the trick. This West Highland White Terrier finds an old jumper and a titbit highly alluring, although the titbit does seem to have the edge!

Stay Sequence 1

Over the next few weeks this and other static exercises will progress from zero to great levels of distance and distraction. It is vital you make sure your dog is firm at the current sequence before progressing.

With your dog in Sit at Heel position at your left side, his front legs in line with your legs, place the lead in your left hand and bring the training collar links to the central point between and tight behind the dog's ears.

Hold your left forearm downwards at an angle of forty-five degrees so that your fist is immediately above the central point between your dog's ears. Fold the lead in your fist so that it is straight in the vertical and at right-angles to the floor. Keep it like this throughout the exercise.

Retaining vertical tension on the lead, stand up straight, command your dog 'Stay' at the same time giving the stay hand-signal with your right hand; without hesitation pirouette to the left and face your dog, toe-to-toe.

At the slightest sign of your dog breaking the Stay or becoming inattentive, check him by sharply twisting your left wrist anticlockwise and command 'Sit', then return the lead to normal tension.

After an interval of between thirty seconds and a full minute, pirouette back to the at Heel position, stand up straight, pause, then relax the lead tension by lowering your left hand down to your side, at the same time praising your dog.

The Stay command and hand signal.

The Stay position sequence 1. The handler stands toe to toe with the dog.

Wait for about fifteen seconds then repeat the procedure a second time. When you return to your dog following the praise, pause again, then terminate the exercise by breaking backwards several paces using the commands 'OK, Dog's name, Come'. Gently pet and praise your dog as for the Play Recall (*see* page 64).

Intervention before the sin is essential in the Stay exercise. If your dog manages to break the Stay, you have been much too slow at reading and anticipating his intentions. The verbal intervention is 'Sit' not 'Stay'.

HOMEWORK
Do two consecutive Sit-Stays as many times as possible each day, terminating the second with a Play Recall.

Stay Boredom

Boredom can be a serious problem in Stay training and must be guarded against. The Play Recall helps to make the exercise interesting for the dog by combining action with a static procedure. Most dogs prefer and are motivated by action exercises. Continual praise in a quiet manner helps to retain the dog's concentration, although, obviously, you do not praise when the dog is thinking of breaking from a Stay.

Kennel Club Regulations for Obedience Competition dictate that any further signal after the last command in Stay procedures must be penalized, and it is generally, therefore, the custom for handlers to remain silent until the 'Exercise over' instruction is given. However, no obedience competition totally excludes background conversation during group Stays, and for this reason it is essential to condition dogs to conversation and other noise during Stay training. Also, for those dog owners ambitious and sporting enough to enter competitions, it is essential to join a good dog training club to complete Stay training in a group format with other dogs and handlers.

Long Down Sequence 2 and Long Sit

Progress to completing Long Downs of thirty minutes and Long Sits of ten minutes, by sitting in a chair with the dog

The Long Sit. This should last for ten minutes and allow for mild distractions. Although reading a book, the handler is alert to what her Airedale Terrier is doing and can intervene with her left hand if the dog even thinks of moving.

The Long Down. This should last for thirty minutes and once again use mild distractions. If intervention is required, pressure should be applied with the left hand against the dog's shoulders.

at your left side facing exactly same direction as yourself, his front shoulders in line with the front legs of the chair. Introduce mild distraction, such as reading a book, watching television or talking to somebody. Do not always use the same chair and location.

HOMEWORK

Over the next week complete one thirty-minute Long Down on the first, third and fifth days and two ten-minute Long Sits on the second, fourth and sixth days. Distraction must be sufficient to make your dog want to move several times and you must be sharp enough to prevent him doing so.

Recall: Come When Called Sequence 1

Play Recall

For the next few weeks do not let your dog off-lead on recreational outings at the park and in open country. With your 7ft (2m) training lead plus an arm's length of approximately 3ft (1m), you can allow your dog sufficient freedom to do all the things dogs enjoy doing within a circle 20ft (6m) in diameter.

Every now and again during outings, when your dog is distracted and least expects you to do so, run backwards away from your dog (still facing him). As you start to retreat, give a quick snap-check on the lead and at the same time command 'Dog's name, Come'. Do not reach out over your dog when he comes to you, but cup your hands under his chin and begin petting and praising, really letting him know how pleased you are.

Next, command 'Dog's name, Heel' and walk on a few paces together, then give your dog his head using the command 'OK'.

Let common sense dictate how often you call your dog in. Repetitions should not be frequent enough to spoil his recreation, which could imprint a negative association with being called. Do not call him unless you are in a position to compel the response.

The Play Recall. The handler runs backwards while facing her dog to motivate the Come When Called response.

The Recall. The handler crouches down to receive the dog. Some dogs at this level of training are reluctant to come close to a standing person on Recall. It does help to crouch down in order to gather the dog in, but refrain from bending over your dog.

HOMEWORK CHECKLIST

Each day complete the following training exercises in brief session format. Also, use each procedure in your day-to-day management and control of your dog.

Distance Control: Two sessions per day with fifteen changes of position between Sit, Stand and Down. Vary the rotation and time interval of commands.

Walking at Heel: Twice each day complete consecutively six Auto Sits, six False Starts and a mixture of each.

Pay Attention: Use plenty of verbal praise to motivate your dog and retain his concentration for the task in hand.

Stay: Two consecutive Sit-Stays twice each day. Terminate each second toe-to-toe Stay with a Play Recall. Duration thirty to sixty seconds.

Long Downs and Sits: On alternate days complete one thirty-minute Long Down and two ten-minute Long Sits, with the dog at the left side of your chair. Use a different chair and location each time.

Play Recall: During recreational outings carry out Play Recalls, running backwards away from your on-lead dog, without spoiling his enjoyment of recreation.

Use the command 'OK' to terminate all exercises.

LIVER AND GARLIC TITBIT RECIPE

Take 1lb (450g) of cattle liver and 2 small cloves of garlic.

Boil together in a saucepan of water until the meat is sealed.

Leave contents to cool in own juices.

Cut liver into small pieces about a fifth of the size of a new five pence coin. Put juice on dog's dinner.

Place liver pieces on a baking tray and bake in a hot oven for about 40 minutes. Take out, turn over and continue baking for another five to ten minutes.

Remove from oven, allow to cool well out of dog's reach. Then store in a suitable plastic container.

The finished product should be like rock-hard pieces of charred plastic which will keep indefinitely. If they are at all soft, they become mildewed in a day or so and unpalatable. This recipe makes sufficient titbits for six months. If you use them up before that time, you are committing the cardinal sin of over-rewarding your pupil.

CHAPTER 9

Lesson 3

Introduction

This week concentrate on increasing the motivation of your dog. Continue to ignore him when you are not training together, and make him work harder for titbits, using them only to reward the Distance Control and Recall exercises. Compel every commanded response.

Distance Control Sequence 2

Progressions this week include standing to face your dog instead of kneeling, and the introduction of clear hand signals. Consistency of the verbal and visual commands is vital. If your dog is slow to get the message when you are standing, revert to kneeling for the first few changes of position, increase motivation, then finish with the handler standing sequence. You must continue to compel each response, using only the necessary tension on the lead, thus avoiding handling your dog as much as possible.

Formal Walking at Heel Sequence 2

This week, four new procedures are added to this exercise: Circles left, circles right, about-turns and straight-line Walking at

Heel. All changes of direction when heeling require a tight lead, held with both hands firmly clamped at the front of your thighs. If, during a turn, you move your hands off your thighs or slacken the lead, you will swing your dog outwards as if on the end of a pendulum.

HOMEWORK

Continue with two sessions each day of this block exercise and fifteen changes of position between Sit, Stand and Down. Increase the distance by standing one short pace away from and facing your dog. Reward your dog with sincere praise and a titbit treat for the first three command responses, then make him work harder for further treats. The timing of the reward is vital.

Circles Left

Start in the Sit at Heel position, with a tight lead and both hands firmly clamped to your thighs. Commanding 'Dog's name, Heel', lead off with your left foot and walk anticlockwise in a circle about 3ft (1m) in diameter. Give enthusiastic verbal

Incorrect positioning of the hands for Left and Right Circles. The handler has allowed the hands to move sideways off the thighs, inconsistent with completing a tight, dog close to handler circle.

Left and Right Circles. All changes of direction require a tight lead, clamping the dog to the handler's left knee. This illustration shows the hands correctly clamped to the front of the thighs. Plenty of continuous praise is required throughout the turn, with the handler remaining in a good upright posture.

encouragement continuously throughout the turn. Complete the full circle, halt, and physically place your dog in the Sit at Heel position, without commanding him to sit. You should be facing in exactly the same direction as when you started. Repeat twice more consecutively.

Circles Right

Circles Right are executed on the spot and call for ballet-style pirouettes. Commence exactly as for the Circle Left, keep your dog clamped to your left knee and praise continuously throughout the turn. Halt facing the same direction as when you started and physically sit your dog at Heel without commanding. Complete three consecutive Circles Right each time you practise them.

About-Turns

About-turns should always be made to the right and are necessary when you want to reverse direction when Walking at Heel with your dog. They are exactly half of a Circle Right.

Straight-Line Walking at Heel

Punctuate your heeling exercises with a few paces of straight-line formal Walking at Heel. Your goal this week is five paces without having to apply a left hand check on the lead. Praise for all you are worth when your dog is in the correct position and cease praising the instant he starts to lose position. Intervention not correction must be your tactic for success.

HOMEWORK

Twice each day practise three consecutive Circles Left and Right on the spot, with an automatic compelled Sit at Heel after each circle. On two separate occasions complete a three to five-minute Walking at Heel drill, include all your at Heel exercises: Auto Sits, False Starts, Circles Left and Right, About-turns and straight-line Walking at Heel. Do not always use the same sequence of commands.

Pay Attention Sequence 2

Concentrate this week on retaining your dog's attention during two exercises: the static Sit- and Down-Stays and Walking at Heel. During Stays, use a snap-check upwards on the lead if and when your dog is distracted and looks away from you. Eye contact between handler and dog is important, but the duration must be built up slowly and at this stage restricted to the occasional glance. Between glances aim your view at just over your dog's head and at all times have a smile on your face. Dogs interpret prolonged direct eye contact as aggression, which causes stress in some dogs and triggers hostility in others. Consequently, canine instinctive eye contact interpretation needs to be modified through repeated pleasurable experience.

During Walking at Heel training do everything you can to keep your dog guessing, and include changes of pace between slow, normal and fast.

Stay Sequence 2

Considerable changes are made between sequences 1 and 2. Instead of being toe-to-toe with your dog, you are now facing him from a distance of half a lead's length. Distraction must remain at a low level and the duration of each Stay should be between a half and one full minute. Other differences include the Return to Dog, with the handler circling anticlockwise close to and around the dog back to Heel position, and the method of checking to prevent Stay being broken, which has now changed to a hand signal and snap-check against the lead.

Start by halving your training lead, placing the ring at the loop end in the trigger-hook attached to your dog's collar. Hold the lead in your left hand and sit your dog square in the Sit at Heel position. Stand up straight, give the Stay hand signal and verbal command.

Without hesitation, circle your dog anticlockwise (do not go out in a wide circle), advance as far as the lead will allow, and turn to face your dog, keeping your hands low. All the time your dog is paying attention praise him in a calm soothing tone of voice. Stop praising when your dog is distracted or thinks of moving, when you must intervene with a sharp check under the lead with your right

The Sit-Stay. The handler remains alert, with the right hand poised ready to strike upwards against the lead the instant the dog thinks of breaking the Stay. The verbal intervention is 'Sit'.

The Down-Stay. Intervention for the Down shows the handler's left foot gently pushing downwards on the lead, towards the tail. There is no need for any great force. Praise and reassurance will help the dog comply by staying put.

hand and command 'Sit'. Note, the verbal correction is 'Sit' not 'Stay'.

After an interval of between half and one minute, return to your dog, circling anticlockwise back to the at Heel position. Pause for a couple of seconds, stand up straight facing front, then quietly praise and reassure your dog, who must continue sitting and staying throughout the whole procedure.

Next, Down your dog with left-hand compulsion against the lead, by using gentle tension directed downwards and backwards toward the dog's tail and in line with his spine. At the same time give the single verbal command 'Down' and signal with your right hand. Proceed as for the Sit-Stay but with appropriate single 'Down' commands when called for. Physical intervention for the Down is achieved by stepping towards the dog,

placing your left foot on the lead under his chin and gently pushing downwards and towards the dog's tail at an angle of approximately forty-five degrees. The instant your dog is Down, quickly step back as far as the lead will allow, and calmly praise your dog. Avoid touching your dog if you can, as doing so rewards him for breaking the Stay.

From this sequence onwards it is very easy unintentionally to train a dog to enjoy the instinctive canine game of manipulating his handler. Intelligent dogs quickly catch on to reversing the pack leader role, when they realize that every time they break Stay their handler returns. Hence the need to place your dog back in position using the lead without physically touching him.

Following the second Stay, break backwards using the commands 'OK, Dog's

The Long Down. A group of dogs perform a Long Down with distraction, at a dog training class run by the author.

name, Come'. Run back further and faster than at sequence 1.

Long Down and Long Sit Sequence 3

Distance is increased this week to 6ft (1.8m) from the handler. Have your dog on-lead and tethered if necessary. Distraction should be at a moderate level. Try to avoid having to return to the dog by using a sharp verbal 'Ah-Ah'! when he first thinks of moving.

Formal Recall and Sit in Front

Two methods are used to teach this exercise: Compelled and Motivated.

Compelled

Have your dog on half-lead and sitting two paces from you. Command 'Dog's name, Come' and quickly, using lead compulsion, gather the dog toward you. Compel the Sit in Front by cupping both your hands under your dog's chin, two fingers of each hand in the collar, and lifting his head backwards. Pull upwards and towards you, bringing the dog close to your body, compelling him to look up, then smile and praise enthusiastically.

Step away and repeat five more times in quick succession.

Do not use a 'Sit' command as the response must be automatic (Auto Sit in Front).

The Compelled Recall. The handler places both hands under the chin and lifts the head back to compel a straight sit.

Motivated

Place your dog in Sit at Heel at your left side on full lead. Place a titbit in your right hand, then give the 'Stay' command and hand signal.

Leave your dog, stepping forward Right Foot first, and move as far as the lead will allow without jerking your dog. Turn to face him. Place both your hands together, arms across your chest. Give the Recall command 'Dog's name, Come', at the same time reaching forward with both hands clamped together still clasping the titbit and lead. Give a slight jerk on the lead if necessary.

As your dog comes towards you, press your hands, still clasped together, against your trunk just above waist level.

Motivate the Sit in Front by raising your hands upwards with titbit to a point at the top of your chest. This will make

The dog drawn in close to the handler and made to look up.
Note: *The dog is no longer shy of eye contact, having made a pleasant association with the procedure. Consequently, although this is a compelled exercise, the actual handling can be quite gentle and in no way forceful.*

The Compelled Sit at Heel. The handler maintains the left hand on the lead, behind the ears, ready to gently compel the dog into the Heel position. Use the single command 'Dog's name, Heel' and follow with motivating, sincere praise.

your dog tilt his head back and, in doing so, sit automatically. Present the titbit to your dog, with both hands, the instant he sits while still thinking 'Sit'.

Complete a Sit- or Down-Stay after all block Motivated Recalls.

The Motivated Recall. The handler holds a titbit with both hands, having motivated the dog into a perfect close and attentive Sit in Front. Praise and titbit must be given immediately the dog sits.

There are many do and don'ts of this exercise. Good timing is essential. Reward begins with praise the instant your dog starts to sit, followed by the treat immediately he completes sitting. Both hands must be used to present the titbit; if you only use one hand you train your dog not to sit straight and to watch your hand instead of looking up at your face. When your dog does look up, smile but do not stare at him. Do not extend your hands or arms over the dog; if you do, he will veer off and try to turn the exercise into a game of 'Catch me if you can'.

On each occasion you formally train Recall, do six consecutively. Watch in case your dog starts to get bored, in which case interrupt the continuity with a brief play session. If your dog sits short, step in close to him as you reward with the treat.

HOMEWORK

Twice each day complete six consecutive compelled Recalls with Sit in Front, and during recreation at the park replace your Play with Motivated Recalls and Sit in Front, rewarding your dog with a treat every time. Provided you do not feed your dog within four hours prior to exercising him, the treats will help to condition the response.

You must be the biggest outdoor distraction in your dog's life. Ensure that your attitude and handling make these procedures fun for your dog by using plenty of reassuring joyful praise.

HOMEWORK CHECKLIST

Distance Control: Two sessions per day of fifteen changes of position between Sit, Stand and Down. Motivate using titbits. Add clear hand signals to the verbal commands.

Walking at Heel: Formal training twice each day for a maximum of five minutes. Include Auto Sits, False Starts, Circles Left and Right, About-turns and five paces of straight-line Walking at Heel.

Pay Attention: Increase motivation and gradually increase eye contact with your dog. Make sure you keep his tail wagging when Walking at Heel.

Stay: Two sets of consecutive Sit- and Down-Stays each day, at low levels of distraction, followed by a Recall and Sit in Front. Distance increased to half-lead length from and facing dog. Also, sandwich block Recall exercises between Stays. Duration half to one minute.

Long Down and Sits: Thirty-minute Long Downs and two ten-minute Long Sits on alternate days. Distraction remains at moderate level, distance increased to 6ft (1.8m) from handler.

Formal Recall and Sit in Front: During recreational outings complete several Motivated Recalls using a titbit plus praise reward for each. Twice each day complete a block exercise of six consecutive Compelled Recalls. The Sit in Front is now obligatory for every Recall.

CHAPTER 10

Lesson 4

Introduction

Continue to ignore your dog between training sessions. This is the last week of compelling every response, but do not allow laziness on your part to mar the continuity of correct response to commands. Your dog is still learning the basics. You must make it fun for him.

Your dog should, this week, begin to solicit your attention by showing a willingness to please. His first attempts at this may be over-excited happy greeting behaviour and, perhaps, even jumping up at you. There are plus and minus factors to such behaviour. The minus is that your dog is trying to make you interact with him and, whilst this may initially be a neutral interaction, with repetition responding to your dog will instinctively elevate his canine self-importance above human status. The plus side depends on the trainer retaining control. Being able to command and immediately compel a Sit or Down response when a dog is excited, without shouting or over-handling reinforces your influence over your dog.

To sum up, you have not trained your dog to Sit or Down until he will do so at moments of great excitement. Dogs responding to a 'Sit' command cannot jump up; dogs leaping about cannot obey a 'Sit' command. Remember that prevention is better than cure and the required command must be given when your dog

first thinks of the sin. Well-timed interventions will ensure that from this week onward you develop ever-improving control over your dog. Repetitive corrections after the event will train your dog to be a hooligan. The timing of commands, intervention and reward will determine which route you travel together; success or failure, the choice is yours.

Distance Control Sequence 3

Continue to use titbits, but sparingly, making him work hard for each treat. This is not an excuse, though, to ration enthusiastic praise for correct responses.

Distance should not be increased this week, as each response must be compelled at slightly higher levels of distraction.

> **HOMEWORK**
> In addition to the twice daily block exercise with fifteen changes of stance between Sit, Down and Stand, give random commands. For example, waiting for a kettle to boil offers an ideal opportunity to give your dog a 'Sit' or other command. Each time he breaks, quickly replace him on the exact spot, facing in the same direction, as he was when you first gave the command.

'St-a-a-a-a-nd.' This Airedale Terrier, despite being coaxed with a titbit into a Stand command, is stressed, will not look at the handler, or accept the treat. His dignity is clearly being damaged and at all costs, training should never injure canine dignity.

The Compelled Stand. This collie cross is compelled to respond to the 'St-a-a-a-nd' command. A forward right hand maintains lead tension and gentle pressure is applied with the left foot against the front of the rear legs. In this case, compulsion is not damaging canine dignity, as the Collie's facial expression shows.

Social Grooming (Stand for Examination) Sequence 1

Stand for Examination is quite an advanced exercise and in the early stages most dogs droop; they adopt a posture of head and tail down with their shoulders and back hunched up, a picture of canine misery. Consequently, extra efforts are needed to imprint the dog with a happy association at being stacked. My own method for teaching dogs to stand proudly has been developed through watching professional dog groomers. Being able to groom your dog enhances your superior rank without damaging canine dignity and, of course, helps to keep dogs in good coat and looking smart.

Stand your dog on a table with a non-slippery surface or on any other suitable elevated surface, such as the second or third tread of a carpeted staircase. Face the side of your dog while he is standing, and put two fingers of one hand in his collar at the side of his neck just behind the ear. Spend five minutes brushing his saddle (the middle part of his back).

The Stand for Examination. This show dog is being posed and trained to Stand for Examination (or stack). Handlers also need to prepare dogs to behave properly whilst under examination at the veterinary surgery.

First reactions to this vary and the dog may demonstrate several behaviour patterns to avoid social grooming discipline. Playfully biting the brush or your hands, growling aggressively, or just playing the fool are the most common responses. If your dog plays up, give him a sharp check on the collar and at the same time growl, 'That'll do'. Continue grooming the saddle with your free hand. If he tries to sit to avoid your attention, intercept him with a hand pushed underneath him and behind his ribs.

Once your dog settles and accepts your grooming, talk to him. Any softly spoken words will do; tell him all your troubles or explain any good fortune that has come your way. Your dog will not understand the words, but will instinctively feel your empathy. After a few daily repetitions, most dogs begin to enjoy being groomed and many handlers find the procedure very calming and therapeutic.

Other members of the household can help to imprint a happy association with grooming in the mind of your dog, if they casually give him a titbit when passing the grooming table.

Two bitches stacked ready at a Breed Championship Dog Show challenging for Breed Best Bitch.

Grooming must always take place at the invitation of the handler, never the dog.

Formal Walking at Heel Sequence 3

Quarter Turns Left and Right are introduced this week. Provided you have completed sufficient training on Circles Left and Right, the progressions to sharp Quarter Turns should not be a problem. However, some thought must be given to handler footwork and the body mechanics of both dog and handler.

When turning right the dog has to accelerate faster than the handler to stay in the Heel position. For left turns the dog is at the central axis of the turn and to stay in position must almost halt and pivot on his front feet.

Right turns require the handler to pirouette on the spot. Remember your Circles Right? Quarter turns to the right are, in fact, quarter Circles Right. Similarly Left Turns are quarter Circles Left, but the footwork for the dog is more intensive and the turn itself is at a sharper angle.

Some dogs will need extra training if Left Turns are to be negotiated in a smart fashion. This includes teaching the command 'Back', which can be achieved by completing the following sequences several times daily over a seven to ten-day period.

Day 1
Sit your dog at Heel at your left side, against a wall. Take two steps backwards commanding your dog 'Back, Back, Heel' and at the same time apply tension with your left hand on the lead parallel to the dog's spine and toward his tail. The wall and lead tension should prevent the dog from turning and compel him to walk backwards. Repeat six times consecutively and if your dog gets it right, give him a big reward and really make him know how pleased you are.

Day 2
Continue as on the first day but in addition, as a separate exercise, complete six consecutive Circles Left. Make each circle progressively smaller. Watch your dog closely and quit with a jackpot reward the moment you see him walking backwards on the rear legs. Commence each

Footwork and commands for the Left Turn.

Footwork and commands for the Right Turn.

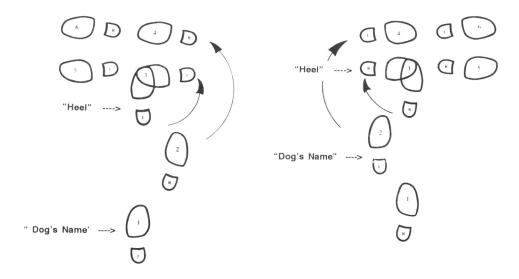

General Notes: The third pace/step in each of these turns (Changes of Direction) necessitates lifting your heel to spin on the ball of your foot.

Body language on the part of the handler is absolutely vital. You must, through good deportment, transmit the message to your dog that you really do know what you are doing.

Learning the actual steps is not unlike learning the steps of a Ballroom Dance, in which respect a little practise without your partner (dog) will not go amiss. It may even with a little luck polish your deportment to Royal Ballet standards. Panache is the operative word.

Get into the habit of keeping your dog at your Left Side and for everyday purposes making all About Turns to your Right. This habit is a safety factor to avoid inadvertently falling over your dog.

Do remember when training your dog to Walk at Heel to use plenty of vocal praise all the time he stays in position. The at Heel position on your left side must become the safest, happiest haven in the world for your dog. *Do not praise* if and when your dog loses the at Heel position.

Footwork and commands for the Right About Turn.

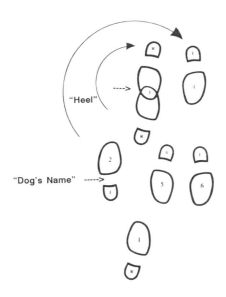

circle, left foot first, with the command 'Dog's name, Heel', followed by repetitive commands 'Back, Back, Back' in a cheerful motivating tone of voice.

Day 3
Three or four times each day train your dog against a chair or table instead of a wall. Concentrate on precision by completing a Quarter Turn Left and Sit at Heel at each corner of the chair.

Days 4, 5 and 6
Introduce Quarter Turns Left to your Walking at Heel sessions.

Pay Attention Sequence 3

During Stay training quietly whisper praise and commands. This allows you to keep plenty of voice in reserve to intervene on occasions when distractions are likely to impair canine attentiveness. Also, the keen attentive dog will watch even more, in case he misses a command or reward.

Walking at Heel training must be a complete contrast. Commands should be given at normal voice level and with enthusiasm, tempered to the degree of instinctive excitability or flatness of the individual dog. Head up, tail wagging, and handler stepping out with natural composure is your goal this week.

The Sit-Stay intervention. The dog has become distracted so the handler intervenes before the Stay is broken. The dog is commanded to Sit (not Stay) with the right hand striking upwards under the lead. Liberal praise should follow the intervention.

General Note: If the dog continually breaks the Stay command, revert to Sequence 1 and work up to 3 in the same session or sessions. This reminds the dog of what is expected and saves a great deal of ineffectual admonishment, allowing more opportunity for reward.

The Down-Stay intervention. This can be done with the right hand against the collar, beneath the chin, applying straight arm pressure by pushing downward towards the tail. Alternatively, the handler may stand upright and apply intervening compulsion with the left foot.

Stay Sequence 3

Continue as in Lesson 2 at half-lead distance from your dog, but increase the
distraction level by having other people
circle him. Practise Stays when other
members of the family are about to return
home and when the postman or other
callers are expected, and take time out
on each recreational walk to complete a
Sit- or Down-Stay.

> **HOMEWORK**
> Twice a day complete two sets of Stays,
> consecutive Sit and then Down. Termin-
> ate the second Stay with the commands
> 'OK, Dog's name, Come', as you run
> backwards five or six paces. Then pet
> and praise your dog. Duration remains
> between a half and one minute.

Formal Recall and Sit in Front

Continue training Motivated and Compelled Recalls as in Lesson 2. For Motivated Recalls reward with a titbit for the
first and last of the six consecutive
Recalls. The other four are rewarded with
praise only. This reward system will
make your dog try harder. Hand movements must be uniform for all Recalls.

Should your dog sit crookedly, quickly
step back one or two paces and manipulate a straight Sit with your hands
clasped together holding a treat. Do not
reward crooked Sits in Front. Should he
sit short, step backwards one pace on your
right foot only, coax him in closer, then
step back to a normal close Sit in Front
with your dog.

Compelled Recalls progress now with
handler in various positions at the front,
to the side and behind the dog.

During recreation outdoors continue
calling your dog when he least expects
you to do so and reward every Recall and
accurate Sit in Front with a treat.

> **HOMEWORK**
> Two block sessions each day of six con-
> secutive Motivated Recalls. Praise each
> Sit in Front. Give a titbit reward for first
> and last Recalls only.
> Two sessions per day of six consecutive
> Compelled Recalls. Call your dog from
> various directions, including from the
> Sit at Heel position on your left side.
> Sandwich all block Recall exercises
> between a Sit- and Down-Stay.

Long Down and Sit Sequence 3

Distance remains at 6ft (1.8m) this week,
but moderate distractions are introduced
by completing Long Downs or Sits at
familiar outdoor locations. Continue the
sequence of one thirty-minute Long Down
on days 1, 3 and 5 and two ten-minute
Long Sits on days 2, 4 and 6. Prevent
any attempt to break by your dog with
well-timed verbal admonishment before
the sin.

General Note

Handlers motivated by success at this
stage are in danger of allowing human
nature to take over in the form of over-
enthusiasm or confidence. They may

become guilty of trying to progress too quickly, or concentrate on the more competent exercises and ignore those which are less successful. None of these exercises are difficult. If you are finding an exercise tricky, question your own approach and technique, as it is probably not the fault of your dog.

Teaching your dog and conditioning his mind to be more receptive to your wishes are the principal goals at this stage. Sandwiching less competent exercises between successful ones ensures that each training session begins and ends on a happy note, which is motivating to both dog and trainer. Progress to a new sequence of an exercise should not occur until your dog is reliable at the current format.

Remember that your dog will learn nothing without praise and reward when he is being good or responding correctly. Make sure you notice and praise all his good behaviour, not just when you are training but also at other times.

HOMEWORK CHECKLIST

Distance Control: Twice daily block exercise with fifteen changes of position. Generous verbal praise, limited titbit rewards. Do random Downs, Sits or Stands when dog least expects. Command once only and compel correct response every time.

Social Grooming: Five minutes each day stand dog on elevated surface and groom saddle. Stand no nonsense, compliment co-operative behaviour with reassuring calm conversation. Have other people pass by and reward dog with a titbit.

Walking at Heel: Continue two sessions per day. Include all Walking at Heel exercises and incorporate the new Left and Right Turns. Dogs who are slack on Left Turns need extra coaching on the static sequences.

Pay Attention: Increase eye contact for the Sit in Front. Whisper commands during Stay training and use compatible vocal reward during Walking at Heel exercises in accordance with the excitability level of your dog.

Stay: Continue two sessions each day at half-lead distance from dog. Increase distractions. Sandwich consecutive Recall training between a Sit- and Down-Stay. Duration half to one minute.

Formal Recall and Sit in Front: Continue as in Lesson 3, but for Motivated Recalls titbit rewards are restricted to the first and last of each consecutive block of six. You must reward every Recall with sincere praise. Expand duration of eye contact. Compelled Recalls now commanded at various directions from dog.

Long Downs and Sits: Long Down and Long Sits on alternate days at familiar outdoor locations. Distance at 6ft (1.8m) and distraction moderate.

CHAPTER 11

Lesson 5

Introduction

This week allow your dog two or three seconds to obey each command of his own accord. When he does so, praise enthusiastically and, on occasion, reward with an unexpected titbit. When he does not respond, apply compulsion without repeating the command. Previous sequences of training may have instilled an automatic response in the handler of applying compulsion instantly for each command, in which case some thought must be given to the two or three seconds delay between command and, if necessary, compulsion.

Motivation is extremely important this week. If your dog has not yet shown clear signs of enjoying training sessions, you have a problem. Recognize this, Research it by reviewing previous training and think about how you are going to motivate your dog. Then Remedy the problem by adding an extra dose of working happiness. I call this the three-Rs policy. The required adjustment may be negative or positive. The negative applies if you have been paying too much attention to your dog between training activity. The positive aspect focuses on the need to increase or improve the timing of rewards. If you have this problem both aspects probably apply, through spoiling your dog with too much familiarity between training sessions and being too

reserved with rewards when you are training together. Remember that each dog is different and sudden change can be dangerous; for these reasons it is impossible to advise a set uniform dosage of reward.

Increase distraction this week. For most exercises this must be a gradual process; some matters however, require a 'saturation' technique. A classic example of this 'take-for-granted' situation is the dog who becomes over-excited in anticipation of a walk the moment you look at his lead. The dog thinks he is taking the handler for a walk and uses every ounce of body language and vocal behaviour to command his subordinate owner to hurry up.

Saturation Panacea

Put your dog on the tag lead and lead him towards the door as if you were going for a walk. The instant he starts to show the slightest sign of excitement, or of taking an outing for granted, do a sharp about-turn and walk away from the door. The instant he stops thinking 'walkies' turn back and advance again towards the door.

Repeat these procedures as many times as it takes to erase anticipation (taking matters for granted) from his mind. Your dog must remain calm and totally under your control. This may take several repetitions on a single occasion, but most dogs quickly get the message and the desired Exit discipline becomes a conditioned response.

Next, attach your normal training lead to your dog's collar and repeat the procedure as many times as it takes to establish full control over your dog. Once you have achieved this, your next sequence is a combination of a False Start and Entry-Exit discipline.

All these sequences must be trained consecutively in the same session and repeated twice daily as a control exercise. Make sure that on other occasions, in similar circumstances but when you are not actually training, you do not under-mine the saturation benefits you have previously achieved. Some dogs will see the light in a single day, others may require ten or more days of twice daily saturation sessions.

Distance Control Sequence 4

Increase duration of eye contact, but be careful to make sure your dog does not show signs of stress or shyness; if he does you are progressing too quickly. Increase distance from the dog to two full paces, nearly the full length of the training lead. Replace titbits with a favourite toy. Terminate the exercise with the release command 'OK' and, with your dog still on-lead, throw the toy over your shoulder and allow him to play with it for a few seconds.

The Entry-Exit discipline. A handler and dog demonstrate the correct Entry-Exit discipline as applied at dog training classes. After a 'Wait' command, the handler passes through the barriers with the right foot first. Following a pause, the handler walks on having commanded 'Dog's name, Heel'.

HOMEWORK
Continue twice daily block sessions of fifteen varied changes of position. Use the toy in your right hand to make your dog more attentive and co-operative through the promise of playful reward. On other occasions, about your everyday business, complete random 'Down', 'Sit' or 'Stand' commands. Remember to allow two or three seconds for your dog to respond correctly of his own accord, before compelling the required response without repeating the command.

Social Grooming (Stand for Examination) Sequence 2

You should by now have eliminated all

*Distance control. This picture shows the increasing distance between handler
and dog; use a similar distance for Stay training.*

attempts at escape and your dog should
enjoy being groomed. Last week you regularly spruced up his saddle in the Stand
position. This week grooming will extend
to the three basic positions and the rest of
your dog's anatomy, including mouth,
legs, feet and rear end. Each day massage
your dog's gums as a precursor to
brushing his teeth in future training
sequences. Cut short the hair between
the foot-pads. Brush and comb legs, tail,
saddle and rear end.

Remember, social grooming is a control
exercise equally important for smooth as
well as long or rough-coated dogs. Most
dogs are hypersensitive to touch on their
legs and rear ends. During the early
stages of grooming these areas your dog
may really play up to avoid your dominant discipline. As in previous sequences

do not tolerate any nonsense, admonish
adverse behaviour in a firm tone of voice,
but make sure you use plenty of reassuring conversation and praise when your
dog co-operates.

The word 'Examination' also has a
practical application in that this exercise
provides a daily inspection of your dog to
discover external parasites, cuts, bruises
or other injuries and skin ailments. Early
detection and first aid often save expensive veterinary treatment.

HOMEWORK
Each day spend fifteen minutes socially
grooming your dog all over, including
massaging his gums and cleaning out
between the foot-pad spaces.

Formal Walking at Heel Sequence 4

This week it is time to sort out individual owner priorities regarding walking comfortably with your companion dog. Idiosyncrasies of circumstance and ambition can differ considerably. The mother with the push-chair having to walk her dog is just one example where major problems may develop without specific training. Another example is the owner who intends to enter Obedience Competitions, as the rules in these regarding the correct Walking at Heel position vary in different countries. Some require the dog to be close to the handler, while others insist on a gap of about 6in (15cm) between dog and handler.

Handler pace also needs to be rehearsed and a compromise achieved to match handler and breed of dog. Obviously small dogs such as Toy Poodles would look very uncomfortable if walked (gaited) at the same pace as a German Shepherd Dog, and vice versa. However, at this stage Walking at Heel must be practised at slow, normal and fast pace to achieve natural deportment at varying pace for human and canine partners. Working happiness is the goal of this training.

HOMEWORK
Train twice daily for five minutes, including all the Walking at Heel exercises and introducing changes of pace between slow, normal and fast. Make sure when street walking to the park for recreation that you do not detrain or undermine all your good work by allowing standards of control to slip.

Pay Attention Sequence 3

Shyness of eye contact should be completely erased during this week. When combined with facial expression, eye contact can mean as much to your dog as any verbal command or hand signal. For this reason your facial expression at any given moment must match the accompanying commands, admonishments and rewards if you are to avoid confusing your dog and in turn impairing his confidence.

Your goal this week must be up to thirty seconds of direct eye contact with a smile on your face and momentary staring stonily as an admonishment to prevent sins such as your dog breaking a Stay.

Stay Sequence 4

Remain at the same level of distraction as in Sequence 3, but increase the distance to the full length of the lead. Note that it is the full length of the lead, not the lead plus an arm's length. However, instead of facing your dog during Stay training take a Quarter Turn Right so that he is facing your left side.

If you are interested in pursuing an Obedience Competition career with your dog, it is important that you complete some regular Stay training in a group format with other dogs and handlers. Now is the time to think ahead on this subject and select some local dog training clubs which you can attend, in the first instance without your dog, to ensure that the club venue and instructors you finally choose are wholly suitable. Having made your choice and, after a few visits, found everything to the liking of yourself and your dog, remain loyal to your chosen fraternity. Disloyalty has a habit of bringing unexpected and sometimes catastrophic results. The exception to this rule is that if you attend a Specialist Breed Club you must also attend training sessions in an all breed environment, as competition Stays are always carried out in groups with a variety of dog types, large and small. Extra training such as this is not being disloyal to your club.

Do not allow yourself to entertain high hopes too soon. Allow yourself simple steady sequences of competitive achievement. Make your first goal and incentive to future success, earning the Kennel Club Good Citizen Dog Award.

HOMEWORK
Complete two block sessions each day of one Sit-Stay followed by a Down-Stay to the same distraction level as in Sequence 3, but increase the distance from dog to full-lead length and stand sideways on to the dog. Also increase the duration to between a half and one full minute. Do not forget to give the release command 'OK' after each Down-Stay then briefly play with your dog. In addition to the block Stay exercises, sandwich consecutive Recall training between a Sit- and a Down-Stay. Remember when returning to your dog to stand up straight, pause, then praise.

Formal Recall and Sit in Front Sequence 4

Continue with six consecutive Compelled Recalls twice a day. Motivated Recalls are still done in blocks of six consecutively, but, instead of rewarding every straight Sit in Front with a titbit and praise, only reward improved responses.

Recall response can improve in several ways: attentiveness, speed of the run in and dog closeness to handler. You must identify each improved response and give a well-timed reward for it. For example, your dog may suddenly run in like a rocket for the first time, but in doing so present a crooked Sit. Reward should come before the Sit in Front, which on this occasion is ignored and excused if your dog is to identify the reward with improved speed. Following each reward for an improved response, interrupt the exercise for two or three minutes by doing something completely different, such as a single Stay exercise, then return to Motivated Recall training.

HOMEWORK
Six consecutive Motivated Recalls twice a day. Reward only improved responses, ignoring lesser responses. Six consecutive Compelled Recalls twice a day.

Long Down and Sit Sequence 4

The distance continues at 6ft (1.8m) from your dog. Progress this week should be made on distraction training outdoors and at home. For example, have other people call your dog during the exercise and admonish any attempt by your dog to respond to another person's command when under your discipline. Go out of sight of your dog for a few seconds, although this does not mean that he is out of your sight. Praise sincerely after each admonishment.

General Note

Reading helps to increase knowledge and the number of published books on canine subjects is legion. Novice dog owners and trainers, having read their third book on the subject of dog training, usually reach a state of total confusion and become demotivated. Restrict your information sources to two books, one on training and the second a specialist book for your chosen breed of dog.

Joining a good dog training club will help to ensure that you do not have too many unintentional hiccups on the way to achieving a high and long-lasting level of control and companionship with your dog. You will make new friends at the club and they will become a source of support, for example, if you need someone to look after your dog during a prolonged hospital stay. You should also be prepared to make a contribution toward club friendships, which should be founded on a cordial give-and-take policy.

HOMEWORK CHECKLIST

Compulsion: Allow dog two or three seconds to obey each command of his own accord. Then compel without repeating command if necessary. Reward correct response with praise in both instances.

Hyperexcitement: Recognize regular instances of your dog becoming over-excited and difficult to control, or taking things for granted. Use saturation technique to modify such undesirable habits.

Distance Control: Two sessions each day with fifteen changes of position. Vary rotation of commands and time interval. Use different locations indoors and out, including some on unfamiliar territory. Gradually increase eye contact and the sincerity of your smile.

Social Grooming: Use the three basic positions for convenience related to part of dog's anatomy you are grooming. Deal with all parts including pads of feet. Keep up the reassuring words and exude happiness and affection.

Formal Walking at Heel: Train two on-lead sessions per day of five minutes duration including all the Heel exercises. Introduce changes of pace between slow, normal and fast.

Pay Attention: Increase eye contact up to thirty seconds duration. Be very conscious that your facial expressions are in harmony with your intent at any given moment and avoid stressing or confusing your dog through being hard-eyed.

Stays: Continue consecutive Sit- and Down-Stays with release 'OK' after the Down. Two Stay sessions per day, plus individual Stays as necessary during your daily routine. Increase distance to full length of lead, dog facing your left side. Duration between a half and one full minute.

Recall, Sit in Front: Continue motivated and compelled block training twice daily, sandwiched between a Sit-and Down-Stay. Reward improved responses only.

Reading: Study a specialist breed book on your particular type of dog. Order a weekly and monthly dog publication from your newsagent. Make sure you learn something new about dogs every day.

Long Downs and Sits: Continue usual alternate daily pattern. Introduce new distractions including short periods out of dog's sight.

CHAPTER 12

Lesson 6

Introduction

By now your dog probably obeys most of the basic commands up to moderate levels of distraction on eight or nine occasions out of ten. The unfortunate likelihood is that he disobeys or ignores commands when control is most important. Provided you are certain that your dog has a good understanding of the basics, verbal scolding is not misplaced when your authority is ignored. For example, if he breaks from a Stay lead him back to the exact spot and replace him in the precise position that he was in before he moved. Use lead control only, not physical contact, to replace him and continuously admonish him 'Bad dog, bad dog', in a low-pitched growling tone of voice, until he is back in position when he must be praised sincerely.

Make sure, in your general training approach, that praise is not diluted by admonishment beyond the ratio of ten praises to one admonishment. If in your case this ratio is unbalanced, you are not yet ready to proceed to Lesson 6 and should instead review and firm up all your previous training.

Canine instinct at this stage leads your dog to think that he can get away with it. Human alertness has to teach him that he cannot and that it is a waste of effort for him even to try.

Distance Control Sequence 5

Continue twice daily block training with fifteen positional changes. This week introduce variety in the time interval between commands within each training session. Sometimes make rapid changes between commands and on other occasions stick to the variable interval of between two and thirty seconds. Admonish kindly any attempt on the part of your dog to anticipate a command. The distance remains the same, two full paces from the dog.

Another change is to introduce a longer lead for outdoor recreation; the commonly used extending leads which automatically retract are ideal. Give random

> **HOMEWORK**
> Two block sessions per day, two paces from the dog, with fifteen changes of position. Introduce rapid changes for some, but not all sessions to sharpen your dog's responses. Your dog may try to anticipate the next command, which gives you the opportunity to turn the exercise into a playful game of wits. During recreation, command and compel if necessary the occasional Sit or Down when your dog is some distance away on a long lead. Increase distance gradually.

single 'Sit' or 'Down' commands when your dog is about 30ft (9m) away and least expects a command. Obeying the command must be quickly acknowledged, by going to your dog and giving him praise, a titbit, and a few seconds to play with an object of attraction (toy).

Retrieve Sequence 1

Although a different exercise to the Recall, there are similarities between the two. Both exercises require the dog to Sit in Front, but in the Retrieve the dog presents an article to hand on the command 'Thank you'.

Several single exercises are linked together to form a complex drill, commencing with your dog on a halved training lead in the Sit at Heel position. Command the dog 'Wait', then throw a toy along the ground to a distance of about 8ft (2.5m) directly in front of your dog. Pause, then command 'Fetch' or 'Seek' and walk the dog to the toy, using your left hand on the collar to keep him tight against your left side. Plant your left leg beside the toy so that your dog has to turn for the Pick-up, and verbally encourage him to do so. The Pick-up is more certain if the dog has been teased with the article for a few seconds before starting the Retrieve drill. The instant your dog picks up the toy, run backwards to the location from which you began. Sit your dog in Front for the Present by cupping your hands under his muzzle and take the toy using the command 'Thank you', at the same time placing a finger against the top palate just behind the front canine teeth. Use the released toy to motivate your dog to the Sit at Heel position, then repeat the whole procedure once more.

The Sit at Heel and Wait. Set the dog up, having teased it for a few moments with a favourite toy.

The importance of exactness in the Retrieve drill cannot be over-emphasized. Each element must be trained to a standard which conditions the dog to know what he is doing. Owners with the ambition to go on to Gundog training or Obedience and Working Trials will find this sequence an excellent foundation for more advanced training.

The drill can be broken down into six elements and it is useful to examine each technique individually.

Sit at Heel

The dog must be facing the same direction as the handler, looking up expectantly, attentive and alert. His front legs should be straight.

Planting the article. Instead of throwing it, the handler leaves the dog and plants the article. This provides an excellent distraction and reinforces the Wait command.

The Pause. Following a pause, the handler returns to the at Heel position, commands the dog to 'Fetch' and walks out for the Pick-up.

Walk Out

This is later known as the Run Out. This must be straight and on a short lead to prevent the dog running ahead of the handler and to condition for cautious Out Runs in more advanced sequences.

Pick-Up

This must be clean and, once picked up, it is a cardinal sin for the dog to drop the article. Verbal encouragement and continuous praise are vital at this level

The Pick-up. With the left leg forward and a short lead, the handler compels the dog to turn for the Pick-up.

of training the Retrieve. Whether in formal Retrieve training or on independent occasions, whenever your dog brings an article to you never admonish or use a negative command to collect the article; hence, 'Thank you' instead of 'Leave'.

There are exceptions to this rule, especially with some terrier breeds, which, being of a dominant nature, hang on to the article as if their life depended on it. Other inducements are necessary in this instance, such as commanding 'Leave' and at the same time exchanging the article for a tasty titbit. Apart from this, using the ignoring strategy and reinforcing the Long Sit and Down responses to teach the dog his proper place in the social dominance order is called for.

Ideally, you should not commence Retrieve training until your dog has learned his proper place in your domestic pack.

Run In

Once your dog has picked up, you must run backwards as fast as you possibly can to your starting point. If you return too slowly you may cause your dog to sin by chaffing the article. Running dogs usually hold the article carefully, as they cannot normally run and mouth the article at the same time.

Present

The dog must Sit in Front, square to the

The Present. The handler runs backwards to the starting point. Providing Recall training has been thorough enough, the dog should Front (sit facing the handler) automatically.

Giving to Hand. The dog is ready to give the article on the 'Thank You' command. It is a cardinal sin for the article to be dropped.

> *General Note: It is advisable not to perform more than two consecutive Retrieves on any one occasion during training/learning sequences. Once the article has been picked up, the run backwards must be at a pace which precludes the dog from constantly chomping on it.*

handler, and look upwards, tail wagging, then release the article to your hand without resistance on the command 'Thank you'. The article should not be damaged or tooth-marked or dropped.

Heel

Following the Present, on the separate command 'Dog's name, Heel' or 'Finish' the dog must go to the Sit at Heel position, swiftly and smartly, look up and be waiting expectantly for the next command.

HOMEWORK
During recreational walks with your dog do several on-lead Retrieves. Do a hundred a day if you so wish, but if you do more than two at any one time you run the risk of boredom creeping in and your dog losing interest in this highly motivating game. Eventually your dog will be required to retrieve a variety of objects and materials; for the time being, however, use a favourite soft toy and do not play tug-of-war with *your* Retrieve article.

Social Grooming (Stand for Examination) Sequence 3

By this stage your dog will probably have become conditioned to enjoy being groomed and will start to give both you and others invitations to groom him. Remember, grooming and petting must be at your invitation only, never the dog's. Use the procedure as a reward for conformity in other training exercises.

Massaging his gums can now be expanded to brushing the teeth with a proprietary canine toothpaste purchased from any good pet shop or veterinary practice.

Your dog's toe nails require regular attention, but most pet dog owners fight shy of cutting their dog's nails and pay a groomer or veterinarian to do it. This reluctance stems from the fact that cutting the nails too short can be painful for the dog and cause profuse bleeding. This is because each nail has a nerve which terminates about halfway down and a blood vessel which travels almost to the end of the nail.

Only the extreme tip of the nail should be clipped, using a pair of plier-type canine nail-clippers. Do not use guillotine types of clipper, which are inclined to split the nail. The pointed nail tip is diamond hard, but once this is removed the remaining nail is quite soft and can easily be filed flat with a fine rasp or quality emery-board. Some dogs have naturally flat nails and do not develop hard points, in which case only the filing procedure is necessary. Long nails distort the spread of the feet and, in the long term, cause all sorts of leg and foot maladies.

Formal Walking at Heel Sequence 5

This week concentrate on improving your own deportment and progress to controlled Walking at Heel road work. Instead of looking down at your dog, develop a head-up stance and feel for your dog's correct position. Shops with full-length windows are an excellent aid to observing your own and your dog's reflection.

Practise the policy of not doing what your dog wishes. For example, if he takes it for granted that you are going south, do a rapid about-turn and go as hard as you can in the opposite direction; if your dog wants to turn right, turn left, and by repetition train him that you are in command and make all the decisions.

Walk only at a very slow pace on all straight-line road work, as this will give you time to intervene with a corrective flick of the lead before your dog gets out of position. If and when he does so, you are too late; correction is not only useless, it actually trains your dog to pull ahead.

You must work with a slack lead, except for changes of direction.

Circles Left and Auto Sits are an excellent method of retaining control during road work. Gradually increase the num-

ber of paces between each Auto Sit. During recreation call your dog in every now and again to complete about twenty paces of straight-line Walking at Heel. Do not as yet let your dog off-lead outdoors; as an intermediate step to off-lead training you can use an extended lead.

Pay Attention Sequence 4

Continue as in Sequence 3, but through practise improve your communicative skill using just eye contact on occasions when circumstances allow. Love has a language all of its own, signalled silently through the eyes and by touch. Provided your dog is comfortable to control in most situations, it is time to take love out of your back pocket and start communicating affection in measured doses. Do not be over-lavish, though, with your affection; if you are you may induce separation anxiety and make matters difficult when you have to leave your dog on his own.

Pay Attention. Handler and dog in perfect harmony, combining control, eye contact and working happiness. What a team!

Stay Sequence 5

Inventing new distractions is the priority this week. The distance remains at full-lead length, but if necessary reduce the distance until your dog is firm at distraction Stays. Continue twice daily consecutive Sit- and Down-Stays at familiar and unfamiliar outdoor locations. At home train Stays when distractions such as the postman or other callers visit, when you

Distraction Stay. A lady handler proofs the dog to the Stay command, practising the Down-Stay in a pause box. A windy day, flapping skirts and a stand-in partner provide suitable diversions.

are on the telephone, vacuuming or sweeping the floor. Ask a partner to distract your dog, even call him by name. Remember, though, that you must read your dog, anticipate the moment he first thinks of breaking Stay, and intervene before he does so with a sharp 'Ah!' or 'No' before he actually moves. Gradually increase the duration from two to three minutes.

> **HOMEWORK**
> Twice daily consecutive Sit- and Down-Stay sessions. Use your imagination to invent new distractions. Train indoors and outdoors in familiar and unfamiliar locations. Terminate each Down-Stay by running backwards further and faster than in Lesson 4 and rewarding your dog with play and very occasionally a titbit.

Formal Recall and Sit in Front Sequence 5

Cease block Motivated and Compelled Recalls. Each day carry out several random Come When Called exercises indoors, calling your dog from one room to another. During recreational walks on an extended lead call your dog in from distances up to 20ft (6m) away and limit his wandering to that distance. The idea is to imprint the habit of quartering, where your dog forages the ground within a 20ft (6m) radius to the left, right and ahead of you. Gradually, over a few weeks of repetition, the distance of each foray can be extended up to 50yd (46m) off-lead without surrendering control.

Make certain that each Recall ends

with a straight Sit in Front and reward improved responses only, with verbal praise and kindly petting, using slow gentle hand movements not patting your dog as if kneading a lump of dough. Some people pat their dogs so hard the poor creatures wander off afterwards in a daze. Touch sensitivity differs in each dog; reward with hand contact can be punishment for one and reward for another. Make sure your hands are instruments of pleasure for your dog, not punishment.

> **HOMEWORK**
> Carry out several indoor and outdoor Recalls with straight Sit in Fronts each day. Reward improved responses only.

Long Down and Sit Sequence 5

If your dog has been firm at previous sequences of these exercises, formal training can now be dispensed with. However, use Long Downs or Sits as appropriate in your everyday management of your dog: when callers visit your home, when you want to put your feet up undisturbed for a while, or whenever you need to retain control in distracting situations.

HOMEWORK CHECKLIST

Distance Control: Continue two block exercises each day. Introduce contrast in time interval between commands: in some sessions make rapid changes, in others prolong the interval between commands. The idea is to keep your dog expectant, but without any attempt to anticipate your next command. During recreational outings practise single individual commands at distance on an extended lead.

Retrieve: Whenever the opportunity arises, carry out two consecutive Compelled Retrieves on three or four occasions each day. If your dog refuses to pick up the article, carry it yourself back to the starting point then give your dog a titbit. Eventually he will get the message. This game is an excellent step towards making you the biggest outdoor distraction for your dog.

Social Grooming: Continue as last week, but extend sessions to include a full manicure of your dog's toe nails. Examine foot-pads, and if dry or chapped apply lanolin sparingly. Ask as many people as possible to go over your dog, mimicking visits to the veterinarian.

Formal Walking at Heel: Improve your own deportment this week. Practise solo if necessary with an imaginary dog. Do plenty of road work and observe your bearing and your dog's through the reflection in shop-front windows, or ask a friend to video a formal session, although be prepared for a shock when you view the tape on screen. Pay particular attention to the Auto Sit and False Start exercises, as Sit at Heel next week will be the last command of the Recall and a finale to the Sit in Front.

Pay Attention: Improve eye contact communication at every opportunity. Make sure your stares and glances imprint your dog with understanding not stress.

Stay: Continue Sit- followed by Down-Stay, twice daily at full length of lead. Introduce new distractions. Train indoors and out at familiar and unfamiliar locations. Duration two to three minutes.

Recall, Sit in Front: Cease Motivated and Compelled block Recalls. Carry out random Recalls and Sit in Fronts indoors and out, at familiar and unfamiliar locations. Your goal is to drop or sit your dog at distance in an emergency. Imagine a dog is off-lead and about to fly across a busy main road, his only chance of survival is an immediate response to 'Down' or 'Sit'.

Long Downs and Sits: Discontinue formal training on these exercises. Use whichever position is appropriate on and off-lead in everyday control situations as frequently as circumstances require.

CHAPTER 13

Lesson 7

Introduction

During this week your dog may reach what is known as his learning plateau, losing his conditioned responses, thinking about his response to commands and, in turn, becoming confused. This set-back lasts for seven to ten days, and experienced dog trainers understand and welcome it as an opportunity to revise basic training. Other names for this stage are patience week and, in dog training classes, drop-out week, when inexperienced students lose faith and believe their previous confidence has been totally misplaced.

This set-back occurs in any training programme, human or canine, and your policy must be to remind the confused dog of the correct response to each command. Go back to the first sequence of the problem exercise and in the same session, a little at a time, work through each sequence up to the current level of training. Having the time, patience and understanding to repeat previous training is critical to success, and this week is the most important – the pinnacle of learning the basic commands and establishing control discipline. Physical punishment has no place in any sequence of dog training. During the learning plateau even a harsh 'No' can induce a host of future undesirable behaviour problems.

During the next three weeks the correct response to basic commands must become permanently imprinted in the dog's mind. Imprinting in the canine mind takes place through the association of inducements, in this case linking a visual and sound signal to each conditioned response. For this reason hand signals must be clear and demonstrative. Once the association of two inducements is learned for each command, your dog will respond to either if used singly. However, if over a period of months both inducements or signals are never used again at the same time, your dog will become detrained in the correct response.

Distance Control Sequence 6

Continue as for sequence 5 on an extended lead, but increase the distance. If you have problems, revert to shorter distances and gradually extend them again.

> **HOMEWORK**
> Two block sessions with fifteen changes of position each day. Also, during recreational outings carry out single Sit, Stand or Down commands. Make sure you detect any confusion your dog may display and help by showing him the correct responses with a kindly attitude. You need a lot of patience and commitment this week.

The Sit hand signal.

The Down hand signal.

Retrieve Sequence 2

Begin as in sequence 1 with your dog Sitting at Heel on your left side on full length of lead. Command your dog 'Wait', while you plant the Retrieve article 6ft (1.8m) in front of him. Return to him, take the loop of the lead in your left hand, pause, then signal with your right hand and verbally command 'Fetch'. Remain standing while your dog Runs Out and Picks Up. The moment he does so, run backwards and at the same time command 'Dog's name, Come'. Halt for the Present and, with cupped hands under his muzzle, take the article commanding 'Thank you'.

Use the lead to prevent your dog running off, but if you jerk it during the Run In your dog will probably drop the article.

Fig 79: The Stand hand signal. Hand signals must be clear, with fingers together and thumb tucked in. Always give these with the right hand, with the arm fully extended if facing the dog. Dogs are inclined to droop when commanded to Stand. An enticing object in the left hand helps to improve motivation and working happiness.

Social Grooming (Stand for Examination) Sequence 4

You should be completely familiar with this procedure now. However, do not become complacent as improvements can always be made. Also, if you drop your concentration and become indifferent during grooming sessions, your dog will regress and resent the change from a playful activity to a working chore.

Concentrate this week on giving grooming an abundance of pleasurable

association. While it is not policy to spoil a dog, grooming is the exception. Your dog must be made to feel important, to stand proud in the Stacked position for his breed standard. Use plenty of conversation in a tone of voice which motivates him, be generous with titbits, and also ask friends and other members of your family to give your dog treats and examine him all over.

Formal Walking at Heel Sequence 6

Provided your deportment is up to standard and your dog now walks comfortably in the at Heel position, you can progress to familiarizing your dog to the street with plenty of road work. Remember not to over-exert puppies.

Training for road crossings is a priority this week. Use a single Auto Sit at the kerb for each and every road crossing. This applies regardless of whether there is traffic or not. Your dog must sit at the kerb every time.

Roundabouts at busy junctions represent a golden opportunity to make your dog aware of traffic. When coming to a kerb edge, Auto Sit your dog; as an approaching car gets nearer to you take one or two steps backwards and re-sit your dog. Do not make a big fuss of the procedure. Repetition will in time condition your dog to have a healthy respect for traffic, without which many dogs never come to understand that motor vehicles cannot stop instantly.

Country dwellers can teach their dog traffic sense by using narrow country lanes. At certain times of the day approaches to riding schools, animal feed wholesalers and so on become busy with visiting vehicles. Regularly walking your dog towards approaching traffic and stepping sideways on to the verge, allowing each vehicle to pass, will, with repetition, imprint the essential road safety message.

Traffic sense is not your only goal this week, you are also training your dog to be well-mannered and disciplined in public places. You achieve this by having the power of command and confidence to make your dog believe you deserve respect and by having the foresight to intervene before correction becomes necessary. Handler attitude is important; even when admonishing sinful canine behaviour, retain a dignified sense of humour and avoid harsh handling at all costs.

HOMEWORK
Concentrate on teaching your dog road safety at busy junctions or in country lanes. Outings must be twice daily within your dog's early twelve-hour memory bank for new learning. Also include a visit to your local market on market-day, walking your dog against the flow of pedestrian traffic.

Pay Attention Sequence 5

Introduce plenty of play in all your activities this week, for example the occasional tug-of-war game on-lead, which you must always win. Allow your dog a few seconds of play on-lead with your Retrieve article. Differentiate between Retrieve and play with a command such as 'Yippee' for play instead of 'Fetch'. Games should be brief, less than thirty seconds in duration, and

given as a reward for above-average performance in response to a series of commands. A frisbee is a much safer and more attractive toy than a ball or stick and makes an ideal game if you have sufficient control to drop your dog at a distance.

Stay Sequence 6

You make big advances in Stay exercises this week. Keep distractions high and the duration to between two and three minutes. The distance remains at full length of lead. Instead of completing a Sit- and Down-Stay consecutively, break backwards using the command 'OK' and play with your dog to terminate each individual Stay.

Stand-Stays are introduced this week. The hand signal for this is given with your right arm fully extended at an angle of about 45 degrees from your body, sweeping your hand through a quarter-circle clockwise from the near-side of your dog to just in front of his muzzle. Lead tension, if necessary, must be forwards parallel to the floor and in direct line with your dog's spine. The hand signal sweep should take the same time to complete as the extended verbal command. The distance used for Stand-Stays at this level is one pace from the dog.

Allowing for any confusion your dog may experience because of the learning plateau, you may need to work through Sequences 1 to 6 in the same training session. If this is the case, you have a great concentration of time-consuming Stay training to complete this week, which may not suit some dogs. Stay, being a static exercise, if over-trained can flatten a timid dog and, in extreme cases, cause him to be deeply stressed. Hence the importance of linking play with the termination of each Stay procedure. Also, dilute any depressing effect with a compensating measure of action exercises and human common sense.

Never break forwards from a Stay.

HOMEWORK

Twice daily sessions of Sit-, Stand- and Down-Stays with play between each. Duration between two and three minutes. Make sure you follow the three Rs: Recognize any tendency for your dog to break a Stay, Research the problem by reviewing previous text, and Remedy by working through each Stay sequence to level 6. Also, use the procedures in everyday management to control your dog as circumstances require.

Formal Recall and Sit in Front Sequence 6

The complete Recall exercise ends with the command 'Dog's name, Heel', when your dog must quickly return to the Sit at Heel position and be waiting expectantly for your next command. This is called the Finish.

Introduce and train the Finish this week. There are two ways a dog can Heel from the Sit in Front: anticlockwise and clockwise. The smartest-looking and preferred method is anticlockwise, but each dog favours either left or right and it is best to use the method your dog prefers. The Finish is initially trained on-lead.

The clockwise Finish requires the handler to take the lead close to the dog's collar with his right hand and lead the dog to the right and behind, at which point the lead is changed from right to left hand and the dog sat at Heel on the left side with upward left-hand lead tension.

The anticlockwise Finish requires the dog to pirouette on his front feet and walk backwards on his rear legs. Some dogs catch on to this technique very quickly, others may require some preliminary training in walking backwards. This is best achieved using the Circle Left exercise, normally completed over a circle 3ft (1m) in diameter. Training consists of repetitive Circles Left over several days, gradually reducing the diameter of the circle until dog and handler are able to complete Circles Left as a graceful on-the-spot pirouette.

Titbit rewards for improved responses should now be given for the Finish and the Sit in Front. Generosity can be increased for a few days, then gradually reduced. During this exercise the toy must only be used to reward the Finish, not the Sit in Front.

HOMEWORK

Twice daily block of six consecutive Recalls, with automatic Sit in Front and separate command 'Dog's name, Heel' to finish the exercise.

During recreation allow your dog to range free in safe areas with tag lead attached. Do some random Recalls and use the tag lead to compel the Finish. Make things fun for both you and your dog.

Long Down and Sit

Continue using either exercise as and

when necessary in your daily routine. Introduce these control exercises to situations in the park by tethering your dog and going for a short walk. Another ideal situation is when you are at dog training class and you go for your break. Command your dog 'Sit' or 'Down' at the left side of your chair, fetch your refreshments and return, quietly keeping him in the commanded position until you have finished your snack.

HOMEWORK CHECKLIST

Distance Control: Block exercise twice each day linking visual signals and verbal commands. Also, on recreational walks give random single commands with the dog on extended lead. Pay particular attention to achieving good response to 'Down' when your dog is distracted and about 6–10ft (2–3m) distant.

Retrieve: Train during recreational walks. Two consecutive extended-lead Retrieves, making sure your dog turns for Pick-up, Sits in Front for the Present and goes to Sit at Heel on command. Play with him for a few seconds after the second Recall. Repeat twice more on each outing with an interval of recreation between repetitions. Revert to Sequence 1 if responses are not up to standard.

Social Grooming: Fifteen minutes all-over grooming each day, paying particular attention to feet, toe nails and examining throat. Reinforce pleasurable association with 'Sit', 'Stand' and 'Down' commands. Dog should Stand for Examination by other persons. Duration two to three minutes. Make grooming a pleasure for your dog and relaxation therapy for yourself. Improve communication by talking freely, relating your happy experiences and your troubles. Your dog scents your emotions, so milk your dog's empathy – doing so is the elixir of mutual trust and understanding between handler and dog.

Formal Walking at Heel: Twice daily road walks teaching road and traffic sense. Correct all transgressions with snap-check on lead and verbal admonishment followed with praise when dog responds correctly. Puppy policy is walk ten minutes, rest fifteen.

Pay Attention: Interrupt all training sessions with a few seconds of play as a reward for doing well.

Stay: Train two formal sessions each day, also use Stay commands as control procedures in everyday situations. Distractions high, locations familiar and unfamiliar, duration between two and three minutes. Break backwards and play after each individual Stay. Stand-Stays only one pace from dog.

Formal Recall and Sit in Front: Research the best Finish clockwise or anticlockwise then train accordingly commanding 'Dog's name, Heel'. Formal twice daily blocks of six consecutive Recalls with Finish. During recreation allow intervals of free ranging with dog on tag lead only. Use tag lead to compel Finish. Reward with titbits and toy.

Long Downs and Sits: Use as necessary for everyday control and management of your dog. Seek out new distractions on familiar and unfamiliar territory.

CHAPTER 14

Purposeful Training Games

Search by Scent

Scent is the most useful canine talent and the means by which dogs take in a considerable amount of information. Most owners coming home to their dog experience the way he enthusiastically smells their shoes and clothing, which is his way of discovering where you have been. Dogs enjoy using their noses and the trait can usefully be manipulated to serve human needs.

Recreational outings on open land offer ideal opportunities for training a dog to search out objects and people. You should realize, though, that you do not have to teach a dog to use his nose, he knows how to do that from the day he is born. Enabling owners and their dogs to have greater enjoyment together is the object of scent training here. Those who wish to complete formal scent training to Home Office or Competition levels will need to read a specialist book on the subject and train under the direct supervision of an experienced instructor.

The system of teaching a dog to search with his nose is basically an expansion of the Retrieve. The only difference is that the article is hidden. There are two essential rules to this training:

1. Your dog must never be allowed to fail a search.
2. Your dog must not be allowed to run on the outward leg of a search.

Training begins with two pieces of dowelling about 8in (20cm) in length. Wrap and secure to the centre of each, a piece of material similar to the cloth from which your Retrieve article is made. Tease your dog for a few moments with a piece of dowelling, then complete one Retrieve with it to make sure that your dog is keen. Next, tell him to 'Stay' and plant one piece of the dowelling some yards away in long grass out of his sight, placing a liver and garlic titbit (*see* page 66) on or by the dowelling. The dog must not see where you hide the dowelling. Keep the second piece of dowelling in your back pocket. Return to your dog and command 'Fetch' or 'Seek'.

The first few times you complete a search your dog will not have a clue what you are doing. Give him the full length of the lead and continually encourage him to 'Fetch'. Whichever direction he takes off in, you must cheat by surreptitiously guiding him to the dowelling and the tasty reward. Your dog must believe that he is entirely responsible for discovering it. Let him know how clever he has been with plenty of excited praise. Repeat three or four times during each outing.

When your dog is competent at this level and able to find the article without any assistance from you, replace the dowelling with a bunch of keys held together on a ring with leather tag attached. The keys should be old ones, no longer in use. You must have two identical articles, as the occasion is bound to arise when neither you nor your dog can find the dowel or key ring; then, without letting your partner realize, secretly drop the reserve item and ensure the search ends successfully.

The next advance on this exercise is to continue using the key-rings, but remove the leather tags.

When your dog finds an article he will develop his own method of signalling the find. Some dogs just wag their tails and look happy, some point like a Pointer, some bark, others pick it up, if practical, and give it to hand. Ideally, with safe articles, the latter is best in most circumstances.

Having completed the above training sequences, you will have taught your dog to retrieve wood, cloth, metal and leather containing your scent. The practical applications of this become apparent on the occasion when you have lost your car keys on open ground and are unable to find them yourself. This may not be a common occurrence, but in my own experience the talent has served its purpose in finding a fishing rod shortly after it was stolen, together with the thief, and saved a car from the salty soaking of a fast-flowing tide. More importantly your dog will enjoy the learning, playing the game and the rewards received for his scenting prowess.

Hide-and-Seek

Hide-and-Seek is another worthwhile game although it does require an assistant. The same principles apply as with the search. You must know where your assistant is hiding, your dog must not. Cheat during the early sequences, as with the dowelling. The hidden person must be the only one to reward immediately with a treat the moment the dog makes contact.

When searching for a person, the procedure is termed tracking, and your dog must be 'given scent' at the starting point of the track. The person acting as the target, out of sight of dog and handler, must drop an article, usually a piece of cloth containing their hand scent, at the starting point which is marked by a post, stick or other identifiable item. The cloth must not be contaminated by other person's or creature's scent. It is also necessary, during early sequences, for the target person to scuff the ground for a few yards as they set off for the hiding-place previously agreed with the dog handler.

Everything is now set for a successful outcome. The dog identifies the route taken by the target person via the cloth, disturbed ground or vegetation, and by wind-blown scent, if down-wind from the target. During early training cross and head winds have a negative effect by avoiding the need for a dog to use ground scent.

Speed, although important, is not the critical factor in search of track training; reliability comes top of the list. It is no use having a dog that takes off at a great rate of knots on the out run. Many are the times an on-lead dog is seen running flat out with his handler clutching the lead with both hands, body almost airborne and parallel to the ground. Although the dog leads in search situations, he must remain under control. The very start of a track and the instant your dog identifies the location of the target person are the occasions when you are most likely to lose command. At this point, use your dog's name to remind him that you are there.

Fishing

Dogs who have a natural liking for water and live with their owners by the sea can, with a little luck, be taught a marvellous game. On sandy flat levels of the shore-line, flat-fish can become marooned in the residual pools when the tide ebbs. Sweeping tidal pools with a push-net often produces the odd flat-fish or two. When you carry out this leisure activity in the company of your dog, you will find that it does not take many repetitions for him to demonstrate canine superiority over a push-net. Once the penny drops in his mind, the number of catches increases handsomely, and a full creel of fish caught by your dog is worth more than all the rosettes and trophies it is possible to win. What is more, you have proof that you are a team in a million, and dog training really is fun.

CHAPTER 15

Where Do We Go From Here?

Canine Reasoning

Two further weeks of training should follow the completion of Lesson 7 in order to imprint desired responses in and erase undesired behaviour from the permanent memory of your dog. This process can be reinforced by updating trainer attitude to competitiveness. From now on, instead of reinforcing human dominance over canine, embark on a lifelong voyage of fun-loving repartee with your dog by beginning to introduce subtle changes of technique to make him think and concentrate.

By doing this, it is possible to destroy completely the myth that dogs are not capable of direct thought and reasoning. Although canine behaviour is largely instinctive, dogs are able to solve small mental problems. They can even ask questions when attempting anything new, by looking at their handler for guidance with regard to what is expected. Simple changes to the format of basic exercises clearly demonstrate the reasoning power of an individual dog. For example, when doing a Recall, instead of facing your dog sometimes stand with your side or back to him. Some dogs respond with absolute confusion, others hesitate and think things out to arrive at the correct solution without further

guidance from their handler. Another example is, with your dog in Sit at Heel position, move your left foot forward one pace but do not actually start to Walk at Heel. If he starts to move, laugh with but not at your dog and retort 'Caught you there, Dog's name'. If the dog stays, praise him reassuringly for not being tricked. Such games and logical tests act as an aid to man and dog working together as a team, with and not just for each other.

Proofing

On some exercises the length of time now needs to be expanded. Taking the Stay exercise as an example, if in Competition your dog has to perform five-minute Stays he must be trained to stay for ten minutes or longer.

Future training must also include increased distractions. Distraction training must subject your dog to a variety of disturbing influences, such as throwing a ball along the ground in front of him, circling him with another dog, using a walking stick or umbrella, hearing marching band music, or other people calling your dog and trying to make him break a Stay. Indeed, you can use any practical distraction which comes to mind. The term for this training is proofing.

Whistle Training

It is now time for those who intend to train their dogs to the whistle to link visual commands with the chosen whistle signals.

There are two types of whistle that can be used for dog control: the silent whistle, silent to the human ear, that is, but audible to the dog; and the hail-a-cab type which can be clearly heard by man and dog when they are several hundred yards apart. The latter type is best in my opinion, as the exact inflection of each whistled signal can be heard by both the handler and the dog.

Start training with the Auto Sit, introducing a short, sharp bleep on the whistle at the exact moment your dog sits as you halt. Several repetitions over a couple of days should be sufficient to tie the association with this new signal. This is not a contradiction of the eight week learning cycle on new procedures, as the dog has learned the Auto Sit and only requires familiarizing with the new inducement. Keep the volume of whistle signals low at this stage, so that you have plenty of reserve for distant control.

The next sequence progresses to the 7ft (2m) leash. During recreational walks, when your dog least expects it, give a sharp single bleep followed by the verbal command 'Sit'. If your dog does not respond, go to the exact spot he was at when you signalled and compel the correct response without repeating the signal or command.

When you are confident your dog will comply with the 'Sit' bleep on-lead at distances of 7–10ft (2–3m), it is time to go off-lead and train your dog to respond at the same distance. Over the next two or three weeks gradually extend the dis-tance a few feet at a time until you can control at several yards distance.

Similarly, by the same increments, condition your dog to a whistled Recall, using a series of stacatto bleeps preceded by the verbal command 'Dog's name, Come'. The verbal command for both exercises can be deleted once the association with the whistle is imprinted in the dog's mind.

Off-Lead Recreation

If you are confident your dog will come when called, off-lead recreation can be expanded beyond the limit of approximately 20ft (6m). Be careful, though, that you maintain control, as, like a piece of thin elastic, it can easily snap if you allow your dog too much distance and/or distraction too soon.

Coming when called, although an important control exercise, is not as important at this stage as the Emergency Down, being able to drop your dog flat and make him stay when several yards away from you. Work hard and well on this procedure during the next two weeks. Recreation presents the ideal opportunity for perfecting the Emergency Down. Start with the command 'Down' when your dog is walking at your side off-lead, walk on ahead of him for several paces, then call 'Dog's name, Heel' and walk on together for about twenty paces before allowing him further recreation. Sometimes leave your dog in the Down and walk on for a distance of about 20yd (18m) before calling him to Heel.

Good Dog, Bad Dog

Even when all the basics are firmly and

The Retrieve. On unfamiliar territory, training must continue on lead until fully established. At home and on familiar locations, off lead Fetches help towards making training a happy experience for both dog and handler. This Airedale Terrier accelerates into the turn for the Pick-up and Present.

permanently imprinted in your dog's mind, his behaviour will still from time to time have its ups and downs. This is more marked in some dogs than others. Young puppies formally trained before the age of six months may, during their adolescence at ten to eighteen months of age, need a refresher course and a further period of compelled discipline. Adult dogs from time to time become pushy and endeavour to dominate. When this happens it is time to return to formal Long Down and Sits and to make the dog work hard for his dinner, not just being made to 'Wait', but given several basic commands before being allowed to eat.

The words of two great military commanders very much apply to long-term control and management of dogs. Wellington stated that an army marches on its stomach; in relation to the canine mind this means that hungry dogs are usually very biddable. Do not make this a plausible excuse to half starve your dog; just remember not to train or work him on a full stomach. Napoleon directed that an army should be manoeuvred according to circumstance. Related to dogs, this philosophy means thinking ahead of situations, out-witting your dog and keeping yourself in the best state of awareness at all times when working or training together.

Canine Competition

Perhaps you have been bitten by the dog

A dog with basic Retrieve training and conditioned to water and gun completes the recovery of a downed water fowl. (Photo: Steve Gilbert of the Hunting Working Division, Airedale Terrier Club of America)

training bug and wish to go on to some form of competitive sport; the Show Ring, Working Trials, Field Trials, Obedience or Agility in accordance with the Kennel Club Rules and Regulations. If this is the case, a good dog training club or professional trainer are your best options for competition success.

Kennel Club Regulations stipulate that dogs under six months of age cannot be Shown and dogs under eighteen months cannot compete in Agility Classes. However, they can and need to start training in a modified format well before the legitimate ages. For example, dogs destined for the Show Ring need months of training if they are going to Stack (Stand and Show) properly at six months; and Agility dogs need to learn directional control over jumps, at much reduced

Bournemouth Championship Dog Show. One of several classes stacking their dogs for assessment by the judge.

Dog training clubs provide many opportunities for further distraction training and proofing. Here Airedale Terrier Club members condition their dogs to distractions of other breeds and a young child on a tricycle.

Agility training. A group of mixed breeds, on their first day at agility class, practise Walking at Heel and Control with distractions.

height, well before they are eighteen months old.

Whatever your feelings for the future with your dog, on completing basic training you should not hypothetically put him back on the shelf until the occasion takes your fancy. Ambition for continuous improvement and further training is a permanent and wise policy and the key to having a dog that is not only easy to live with, but a lasting source of enjoyment.

Socializing for Charity

Regular visits to busy public venues help to keep a dog properly socialized in the community. When combined with a little fund-raising for charity, the procedure

Obedience Competition. Handler deportment is very important. Whilst training the Return to Dog and off-lead Stays, this handler clearly demonstrates the power of command in a quiet, orderly way.

becomes purposeful in more ways than one. Local hospitals always need additional funds and usually have a volunteer or paid charity fund-raising secretary with whom you should liaise to ensure that you keep within any regulations. Dog lovers often find it hard to pass a collection box when the person holding it is accompanied by a dog of friendly disposition.

The organization Pro Dogs is a registered charity with a scheme for official hospital visiting. The therapeutic value dogs can bring to the sick and infirm is recognized by the medical profession. The financial worth of a good dog and handler is also applauded by sensible hospital managers, who are not slow to advertise canine fund-raising achievements in the local press.

The presence of a well-controlled dog and responsible owner at charitable events also goes some way towards countering the growing anti-dog feeling, both by demonstrating good behaviour and by showing that dogs serve mankind and can give back to the community a great deal more than they take out.

PART 3
BEHAVIOURAL PROBLEMS

CHAPTER 16

Aggression

There are many causes of aggression in dogs, most of which can be avoided with training and proper socialization. Few dogs are natural pugilists; most incidents of dog biting either man or another dog occur as a defensive behaviour, and this is known as fear biting. A programme of confidence building and resocializing usually modifies fear bite behaviour. The psychology involved covers a wide spectrum of factors; to make progress on a confidence shaping programme you may therefore need additional guidance from a canine behaviour specialist recommended by a veterinarian.

High Rank Aggression

Dominance is one common cause of aggression, although dominance and aggression do not necessarily go together. The dog who thinks he is the boss of the household, may, in some instances, become very quick to use his teeth on owners or visitors when, by canine standards, established pack status is transgressed. The dominant character will also, from time to time, use his teeth for no apparent reason other than to reinforce his high rank.

Teaching a dog his proper place in the family unit must avoid direct challenge and subsequent conflict. Aggression treated with aggression will make mat-

ters worse and increase the frequency of incidents. Correct safe remedies to modify the behaviour of a dominant aggressive dog require a programme of gradual change, in accordance with instinctive canine social interaction. Over a period of weeks changes should be made in the following areas: feeding, the dog must be fed last and receive no between-meal titbits; sleeping, the dog must sleep where the owner decides; walking, should be where the owner decides and chooses; resting, the dog should be prevented from lying in corridors about the house and from getting on furniture. The dog should also be ignored for two or three weeks except when he is being trained, thus making him feel unwanted. Control training should be given, using Long Downs and Long Sits, and Entry-Exit discipline should be revised.

Social Grooming

Instances of aggression can occur if you try to pet or groom high-ranking dogs uninvited. This explains why on one occasion a dog will growl when he is touched, yet at other times be perfectly receptive and happy.

Most dogs protest when first subjected to social grooming and try to evade the discipline, but after several firm repetitions they start to enjoy the procedure. Owners of smooth-coated breeds may erroneously believe regular grooming is unnecessary. Aesthetically it is not as important as with long-coated dogs, but regular grooming is vitally important in teaching a dog his proper place in the social order.

Regressive Problems

Some behaviour patterns can be changed in a single experience using mental shock followed by reward. It is not wise to use this method, however, to correct high rank or fear aggression as the dog is likely to regress to his old ways in time. Aggressive dogs will respond to the shock method but easily regress, and antisocial behaviour is extremely difficult if not impossible to counter-condition if the dog has a history of regression after two previous courses of rehabilitation. Better to make gradual changes, lowering the dog's position in the 'pack' by reinforcing your own. Thus, again, you must be seen to eat first, to sleep in a more elevated position, and generally to bestow favours when *you* feel like it, *never* when your dog demands.

It is important to note that this rule applies only to cases of established aggression, not to the training of puppies or dogs. For example, if a puppy is mouthing, a shock admonishment when its teeth make contact with human skin or clothing followed by praise will usually prevent a recurrence of the sin. The method should be a harsh growled 'Leave'. The moment the pup hesitates verbal praise should be given and a hand should be presented to the pup, who will normally gently lick it. The pup can also be praised for this and so will learn that licking is allowed but teeth must not touch a human being.

Fear Aggression

Some dogs suffer a primitive streak of shyness towards humans or other dogs, or both. Such behaviour traits may be of genetic origin, but may also result from adverse environmental experience or, more commonly, from removing a puppy from the litter at too young an age before it has learned it is a dog.

Some dog breeding establishments are totally staffed by either females or males, and a puppy will therefore only experience single human gender stimulus which may cause problems later. Tactile stimulation by the dam and both human sexes is important from the start. Early exposure to multi-race situations is also advisable during socialization to prevent possible prejudiced behaviour later on.

Puppies who miss out on early social imprinting can, for the rest of their lives, be reserved and even fearful of men or women, whichever the case may be, even when they live in the same household and as adults they may demonstrate extreme aggressive and prejudiced behaviour.

Modifying Fear Aggression

Regardless of the cause or origin of fearful behaviour and shyness, dogs who suffer from this can be quick to bite without warning if cornered or approached too closely. They feel threatened and you must understand that at such times they are absolutely terrified.

Fear and shyness can in most instances be adjusted by a programme of confidence building, which is fully described in Chapter 17. Generally, it takes understanding, patience and commitment to rehabilitate a nervous dog to an acceptable level of behaviour.

Diet and Aggression

An unbalanced diet can cause a variety of behavioural problems and attention should therefore be given to your dog's diet. Avoid additives such as aniline dyes and preservative chemicals and take into account the differences in body chemistry between dogs, causing some to become aggressive on a high protein intake, and others on a low protein diet. The effect quantity and content of food have on your dog's behaviour can only be ascertained by careful observation.

Remember, if changing your dog's diet, that it may take him a few days to adjust to it and during this period he may experience scouring (diarrhoea). Therefore all changes in diet must be introduced gradually.

Guarding Instinct

Guarding is another common cause of antisocial problems and dogs with a strong guarding instinct frequently, through lack of proper training, fail to develop any power of discernment between friend and foe. This is often reinforced by human reserve, when a dog mimics the owner's attitude to approaching strangers. Repeated negative experiences can exacerbate aggressive behaviour.

I will illustrate this by using a factual case history. One large heavy breed of dog brought to me for training always showed a friendly disposition when on recreational walks. On or off-lead he never gave other people any cause for concern, despite his size. The owner, on taking charge of this trained dog, came for several weekly lessons to complete more advanced training. During the sixth

visit the owner informed me that during the last few outings his dog had started to growl at passers-by. Owner and dog were taken to my favourite training venue and allowed to walk several yards ahead of me and I was able to observe that the dog did indeed growl and adopt a very macho posture when other walkers came towards him or his owner. After this happened a few times I took charge of the dog and during a half-hour period passed many other people and dogs without incident. The only difference was that whereas the owner did not pass the time of day with passing strangers, I did. Social reserve on the owner's part caused the dog to view strangers as intruders. In my case the friendly exchange of greetings showed him that other people had as much right to the territory as we did and were no cause for concern.

Territorial Aggression

Territorial aggression can be a problem. Dogs allowed on their owner's bed, for example, often bite when being removed. Similar problems may also occur outdoors.

Rover is taken on most days of the week to a fairly isolated location for a run and given the freedom of the great outdoors. Rex is similarly taken by his owner to the same location, but at a different time of day. During their early visits, neither dog goes far from his owner, but gradually, through subsequent outings, their daring and confidence increase the distance of their forays. Each dog spray-scents posts to mark out an invisible boundary claiming the territory as theirs, the problem being that each dog is over-scenting the other's territorial claim and as both dogs are high in social rank neither is likely to be subservient to the other.

One day both owners and their dogs are at the location at the same time. Rex and Rover on sighting and gaining scent of each other quickly become locked in combat. Both owners are shocked and claim their dog has never behaved in such a manner before. Eventually, each departs with his dog, both believing the other to be the guilty party. Sadly, through a single experience, in future each dog is at best likely to attack on sight any dog of similar appearance to his adversary, and at worst will attack all other dogs.

The moral of this is to use several venues for recreation, including some where you will occasionally meet several other dogs and their owners. Have a chat and allow the dogs to play together for a while off-lead under covert supervision.

The Canine Bully

Some dogs are born bullies, but canine mugging is more commonly a learned experience. Patch, whose normal disposition had always been friendly and subservient to high ranking dogs, had a bad experience in the local park one day when a larger dog attacked him without warning. The next time Patch spotted another dog he decided he would have the first bite and the other dog hastily departed from the area. Patch was delighted with the outcome and keen to repeat his pleasurable pugilistic experience, and became a first-class bully.

This story would be very different if Patch had attended group training and play sessions, through which the cumulative experience of friendly interaction with other dogs would override the effect of the occasional adverse encounter.

Genetic Imbalance

Although quite rare, it does happen that some dogs are born trouble-makers, it is part of their genetic make-up. Selective breeding of pedigree dogs for the show ring from time to time causes a particular breed to become over-popular. Disreputable breeders quickly latch on to this, and since their main interest is financial gain they will have little or no thought for the breed's well-being. Especially with the larger breeds, or those with a history of fighting, they will breed from any dog that promises size and gameness, caring nothing for the possible unsoundness of the eventual offspring. Aggression and other behavioural problems consequently manifest as common traits and, just as speedily, the breed loses favour, fashions change and a few dedicated and responsible breeders are left to repair the damage caused to the breed.

Only one course is open to responsible owners of genetic rogues: having the dog humanely put to sleep. This statement is written with some concern, though, because many irresponsible people have had healthy dogs put down through their own lack of commitment, falsely claiming that the dog was a born trouble-maker. Sadly this happens all too often. Remember, all the problems in the world of dogs are of human origin, caused either by the breeder or subsequent owners.

Dog Lungers

Dogs have their own instinctive ways of greeting another dog. Off-lead, left to their own devices, canine encounters usually end with indifference or playful romping. The trouble begins when the dog is on-lead and restricted, as he feels trapped and defenceless. Inexperienced handlers exacerbate the situation by pulling and showing concern at the rigid hackles-up approach each dog at first shows. This is not aggressive behaviour but respectful caution, which quickly turns to tail-wagging if the lead is kept slack. Restrictive handler interference with normal canine greeting can, however, cause both dogs to read the situation as abnormal, which in turn can trigger instant combat. Few repetitions are necessary to imprint lunging behaviour, when the dog leaps forward barking, snapping and snarling as a warning for the approaching dog to keep his distance.

Another cause of lunging is hard or prolonged eye contact in a dog class situation. Many training classes have too many dogs for the particular venue. The group line-up during instruction, therefore, instead of being a single line is a U-formation, which can result in hard-eyed Collies staring stonily at terrier-type dogs. The Terrier subjected to this imposition stores up animosity and waits for the opportunity to put the perpetrator in his place with a sudden aggressive lunge. In this case both Terrier and Collie become lungers.

Lungers can be rehabilitated and made to change their ways, but the variety of possible causes makes it unwise to generalize without actually seeing and assessing the individual dog. If you have this problem, consult a recommended professional trainer.

SUMMARY
Prevention is better than cure
The following rules apply:
1. Make your dog work hard if you use titbits, only giving one after he has obeyed several commands.
2. No senseless petting. Make your dog obey a command or two first, then pet at your invitation only.
3. Never pet your dog for more than a few seconds at a time and finish with 'That'll do' or 'Enough'.
4. Exit-Entry discipline, human before dog. One important exception to this rule is automatic doors in public buildings and on transport where dog and owner must enter together.
5. Have a special soft toy as an object of attraction to your dog. Use it regularly to play 'Fetch' (only two Retrieves on each occasion). The game must be at your invitation, and you must put the article away out of dog's reach afterwards.
6. Never rough-house with your dog. The only game of strength to be played is on-lead tug-of-war. Never allow your dog to win the game.
7. Groom your dog every day. Stand no nonsense with evasive behaviour.
8. Make sure you do your Long Downs and Sits to ever-increasing levels of distraction.
9. Never strike or beat your dog, not even with a rolled-up newspaper.
10. Choose a good dog training instructor, remain loyal and remember that criticism is constructive, not personal.

CHAPTER 17

Fear

Fear Complexity

Some dogs are terrified of motor traffic, as a result of which they may become fearful of other things associated with it, such as light beams, flashing lights and screeching sounds. The further the circumstances from the primary fear inducement, in this case cars, the less intense the fear response. For example, a dog fearful of cars, when resting quietly in the kitchen on a sunny day may, through association, be disturbed and show signs of anxiety for a short period of time when the sun's rays are interrupted momentarily by a passing object. In the absence of the primary fear trigger, motor vehicles, the aversion is much less marked. The same dog shows no anxiety at the approach of the family car, with which he has a pleasant association.

Accurate Diagnosis

Identifying the correct approach of a course for counter-conditioning fearfulness rests on an accurate assessment of the primary cause and related inducements. Psychoanalysis of canines is not possible, so the circumstances which led to the particular phobia can only be guessed at. For this reason, although excellent for many other problems, when tackling fear it is not very useful to consult pro-

fessional canine behaviourists for just one or two hours of counselling at a venue which is unfamiliar territory to both dog and owner.

The person responsible for prescribing the course of behaviour therapy should live with the subject dog for a sufficient period of time to identify fully all the idiosyncrasies of character and circumstance. This will also enable various aptitude tests to be repeated several times, thus making absolutely certain the possibility for error does not exist. After all, integrity demands that the dog is given every possible consideration.

The exception to this is direct fear aggression to people or dogs, the symptoms and causes of which are usually blatantly obvious. However, even then you must look for the non-obvious and care must be taken to ensure that the chosen counter-conditioning method improves social compatibility and does not increase aggression. The adage related to corporal punishment, beat one sin out and drive six more in, equally applies to the kindest of techniques if the choice of method is unsuited to the individual dog.

One classic example of kindness increasing fearful behaviour is when the dog has a hypercompassionate and subservient owner. Rover spooks at something, the owner cuddles the dog and whispers reassurance in his ear. Rover

121

thinks 'Terrific, I'm noticed at last'. During the moment of reward he is thinking 'fear'. Few repetitions are needed to imprint permanently the association 'Mummy only loves me when I'm nervous'. The behaviour would be very different if totally ignored.

Misdiagnosis is often made when naturally cautious dogs are described as fearful. There is a world of difference between fear and caution: fear is an undesirable trait, while caution is highly desirable.

Counter-Conditioning

There are three standard options to counter-condition fearful behaviour: relaxation, saturation, and natural necessity. Hypothetical examples based on factual case histories are given below. Beware: it is not a good idea to believe any method is suitable for a do-it-yourself approach. If you have a fearful dog, consult a recommended professional.

Relaxation

Kelly, a Black Labrador bitch aged three years, had been frightened at ten months of age by a thunder-flash thrown at her by a young boy. Since that time, she went into a state of absolute terror in response to all similar sounds. The periods immediately preceding and following Guy Fawkes celebrations were absolutely pitiful. Kelly would dash to the bathroom, leap into the bath and literally try to climb down the plug-hole. Her fear of thunder equalled that of fireworks, and a thunder-storm in northern France was sufficiently close to her location in Hampshire to trigger adverse anxious behaviour, although not to panic level.

Sedative drugs prescribed by her veterinarian helped at first, but repetitive use developed a tolerance to the drug. Kelly even reached the state where a door slamming unexpectedly spooked her. The crisis came when, out for a walk on-lead with her owner, a car back-fired and Kelly took off with such momentum she threw herself and her owner into the path of oncoming traffic. Screeching brakes and lots of abuse from drivers followed the near-critical incident. Something had to be done.

Kelly boarded at my kennels for some weeks for assessment and treatment. Relaxation became the chosen therapy for her, preceded with a programme of general confidence building to win her trust. During the week before Bonfire Night early each evening she was given a prescribed slow release sedative and, when the first distant explosion came, laid flat on her side and gently massaged, especially around her ears and neck. No words of reassurance, just touch.

Kelly's first response was one of concern, but not alarm, and the benefits of this method were immediately obvious. Repetition the next day began earlier, just after 4 o'clock. Further repetitions were made on each subsequent day and by the sixth day sedation was stopped, and indeed was unnecessary. By then you could tell the time by Kelly, who at 4 o'clock would go to the rug on which she had been laid and of her own accord rest there, totally relaxed. Both rug and Kelly were returned to her owners.

A total cure cannot be claimed as explosions and thunder still cause her to show mild anxiety. Kelly has not, however, regressed over a two-year period and, when street walking, like her owner she is aware of loud incidents, but ignores them.

Saturation

Oscar had a problem with traffic, it terrified him and taking him for walks was an embarrassing burden for his owners. Having him as a boarder was not practical, so over several visits he was assessed and his trust earned.

One hundred yards from my kennels there is a large multi-junction roundabout, with a small green containing a single park bench immediately adjacent to it. For several consecutive days Oscar was taken twice daily to the green and made to do a Long Down facing towards the traffic at peak periods. He was saturated with traffic. Once he began to accept the situation, saturation was increased by walking him clockwise round the five junctions which intersected at the roundabout. Subsequently, walks round the junctions anticlockwise in the face of oncoming traffic confirmed his new-found high tolerance of traffic.

Food was given its place as a reward in the latter stages of counter-conditioning. Oscar was fed twice daily, immediately on return from his outings.

Incidentally, stressed dogs will not eat and some dogs go to great lengths to camouflage stress, especially in group situations. The practice of giving the odd titbit to every dog in a group situation can be the first indication a dog is not relaxed. Although there are, of course, many other reasons a dog will refuse food.

Natural Necessity

Angela, an Airedale Terrier bitch, had been returned to her breeder for being vicious, allegedly for biting the man of her new home. She was eleven months of age. I arranged to visit her at the breeder's kennels. There was no way I could describe her as vicious. Taken for a walk on-lead, she was a pleasure to be out with. The breeder and I came to the conclusion that the allegation of viciousness was probably an excuse for a dog which had worn out the novelty of dog ownership. However, to make sure we agreed that Angela would come back to my own kennels for a while, the intention being to keep her as a house dog in circumstances similar to those in a domestic household. She travelled well in my vehicle.

Everything was fine until she entered the kitchen, which had a ceramic tiled floor. Angela shot under the kitchen table, absolutely terrified. The sight of a person with any item, newspaper, pencil, pen, tea cup or plate, in their hands increased her stress. No verbal encouragement or food would make her even think of evacuating her refuge under the table. Her demeanour was pitiful beyond belief. Force was not an option.

Angela did not eat or even show the slightest interest in food during the first two days. Fortunately it was summer and we were able to leave the back door open. When no one was about she would sneak outside to open her bowels, but the slightest sound made her dive for cover under the kitchen table. This behaviour, however, provided us with the opportunity to leave food in the yard and on the third day she did take the meal put down for her.

Margaret, my wife, and I dined in the kitchen at the table. We followed the policy of ignoring Angela, having decided that if she was going to get over her phobia it would be out of natural necessity. Other than to open her bowels or to eat, she remained under the table for two weeks. She eventually ventured out one breakfast time. Margaret and I eyed each other cautiously, not daring to make a sound, then to the best of our ability we acted normally and paid her no attention.

During the next three months every rule relating to dominance and teaching a dog his proper place in the pack order was broken to lift her self-confidence. When the time came for her to return to the breeder Margaret, who had put her foot down regarding our owning any more dogs, shed a tear or two and put forward a case for keeping her.

More than seven years later Angela is my favourite, although I try not to show it. She gets away with murder, has given us three excellent litters of puppies before being spayed, and to us is absolutely priceless. The only residual hang-up from her original behaviour is that if you have anything in your hand, and I mean anything, she will back off and cautiously stand her ground until you put the article down.

What caused her to behave as she did can only be guessed at; she probably had a bad experience, although this may not necessarily have been the case. As we had no factual case history of events between her ages of eight weeks and eleven months, Natural Necessity and patience were the only options for modifying her behaviour. Whatever it was that triggered her phobia, we will never know for certain.

Homeopathic Therapy

Many dog breeders involved with the show dog fraternity swear to the good effect of homeopathic remedies, especially for modifying stress and fear behaviour in dogs. Certainly the reputation for specific flower-based products has been deservedly earned, tried, tested and proved over many years.

Three flowers which produce products beneficial in the treatment of fear are the rock rose for dogs who suffer very acute fears bordering on terror, aspen, for apprehensive worried dogs, and mimulus for shy, timid dogs.

Summary

When dealing with a fearful dog it is easier to make matters worse than it is to improve or erase such undesired behaviour, however good the intention. The object of this chapter is to reassure dog owners that a great deal can be done to remedy fear problems under the supervision of skilled professionals and to avoid gimmicks and people who simply want to impress with their imagined know-how. The deciding factor for measuring the worth of a counsellor is not by how impressive he is but by the degree of empathy between counsellor and dog.

When dealing with problem behaviour there are two terms in common use to describe different therapies. Counter-conditioning is used when the undesired behaviour needs to be totally eradicated, such as in cases of aggression. Modifying is used for behaviour habits which are desirable, but occur at the wrong time or place and need to be channelled to an acceptable purpose. Examples of this are house-training, and the dog with a strong trait for gathering his owner's possessions. House-training can be modified by teaching the dog to excrete on command at the proper time and place. Dogs with strong gathering traits can be turned into wonderful retrievers or search dogs.

CHAPTER 18

Nuisance Barking

One of the most distressing situations for any householder is incessant barking by their dog; not only is it annoying to the dog's owner, but to the neighbours and in extreme cases the whole community.

Legislation

Your neighbours have the right to enjoy a certain degree of peace and quiet, as far as is practical in their particular community. Their rights regarding the nuisance of loud noise are covered by the Noise Abatement Act, usually enforced by the local Environmental Health Office, but sometimes by the police.

Dog owners should not, however, have their privacy disturbed by futile complaints about the family dog barking. The Law does not state that your dog cannot bark, provided there is good reason to do so. Neighbours only have cause for complaint when barking is incessant, prolonged and senseless.

Environmental Health Officer

Should you have a visit from the Environmental Health Officer (EHO) regarding your dog being noisy, he will probably have arranged observations outside your property on at least a few occasions to confirm and collect evidence that your dog is or is not noisy. The EHO will not be concerned if your dog barks a thousand times a day, if on each occasion someone attends to stop the noise. Only if the dog is allowed to bark unchecked can action be taken.

EHOs have limited powers. Usually, if he decides to act on a complaint the first approach will be a knock on the door to appeal for reason. Visits will be followed up by a letter formally advising and substantiating the complaint. Should noise continue the EHO will certainly consider, after correspondence with you, a prosecution through the local Magistrates Court. Pre-court visits can be in the company of a police officer to ensure that the peace is kept and an inspector from the Royal Society for the Prevention of Cruelty to Animals (RSPCA). During this three-pronged assault not only noise will be taken into account, but any health hazard, including animal excrement and method of disposal, condition of animals, building and planning regulations, to name just a few legislative matters they are within their right to pursue. The consequences do not bear thinking about.

Modifying Noisy Behaviour

Those who are unlucky enough to own a loud-mouthed dog must do a lot of forward planning and take stock of many factors. The strategy of modifying the noise problem basically concerns in-depth supervision. This is difficult, if not impossible, in the household where all the human residents are absent at full-time employment most days of the week.

Observe the stimuli which instigate barking: door-bell, milkman, refuse collectors, car doors closing, fence-chasing passing dogs, the neighbour's cat, and any other inducements. Keep a log for a few days recording barking incidents and their cause, as this will allow you to draw up a strategic plan of action.

From your observations recognize the regular causes, some of which can be removed; for example collect your newspapers instead of having them delivered, install a 'no hawkers or circulars' plaque, and, if practical, lock the front gate to bar callers in your absence. Stopping your dog from barking altogether is not practical, is in fact cruel, and in any case is undesirable as you would not wish to stop a house dog from barking when strangers call. The goal must be to reduce the number of incidents when your dog gives voice.

When leaving your dog on his own, it may help to camouflage other stimulating sounds if you leave a radio switched on. My experience of dealing with removable bark inducements has demonstrated that residual incidents are not necessarily unreasonable or problematic, for example when trouble-makers are teasing a dog with silent whistles, inaudible to human ears but highly stimulating to most dogs. Incidents which continue to be a problem need a direct approach, for example in the case of households which have frequent visitors and suffer a fanfare of noise announcing each arrival and departure.

Have your dog on-lead, anticipate the moment he is about to give voice and intervene before he does so as follows:

1. Give a sharp check on the lead.
2. Command 'Leave' in a deep guttural tone of voice.
3. Covertly drop a tin tray on the floor.

The three interventions must come together in unison, and at the moment of hesitation the dog must be praised. This follows the principle that shock followed by reward changes behaviour in a single experience. Should supervised interventions continue to be necessary, they will require only a harsh 'Leave' command, followed by praise for a correct response.

Dogs who are only problematic when their owners are absent need a hoax approach. Set up a situation to make your dog think you are off to work or shopping for the day, whatever your normal routine is. Set up a baby alarm with the transmitter on an extension lead at a covert outdoor location and the receiver indoors with your dog. Leave the house and surreptitiously conceal yourself. The instant he starts to bark shout 'Leave' into the transmitter, and if the barking stops praise sincerely. This method generally has the required effect which, with luck, may last a long time although it will require periodic repetitions for permanent success.

Indoor Kennel

Portable indoor kennels can have a very calming effect when used to confine a dog on a regular basis for a maximum of two hours each working day and will reduce the incidents of indiscriminate barking. Their use for rest and isolation has already been described (*see* Chapter 5) and they are also ideal when trying to prevent destructive chewing (*see* Chapter 19).

Noisy Breeds

Some breeds of dog are inherent perpetual barkers, especially Samoyed and a few Terrier types. Any dog born with a strong chase instinct is likely to be very vocal. When noise problems originate from selective breeding and are of genetic origin, the effort necessary to modify the behaviour is so time-consuming as to be outside the bounds of practicality. The only solution is to move house to an environment where barking will not be a nuisance to others.

Noisy Dogs in Cars

The family car often triggers a chase instinct and an accompanying vocal chorus. Offending dogs do not always understand that it is the vehicle which is moving; they may see the passing scenery as fast-moving objects, a pack of animals. Fast movement induces chase-hunt-bark behaviour in many dogs. Within the confines of a saloon or estate car chase barking reaches cacophonous levels painful to the human ear.

Remedies

The remedy is to remove the movement stimulus from the offender's view before the behaviour becomes an established habit. Buy a travel crate of a suitable size for your dog; long enough to lie at full stretch and of sufficient width for the dog to turn round comfortably, but in height insufficient by a small margin to allow him to raise his head above withers (shoulders) height. Unlike roosters who need to extend their necks to crow, dogs can bark when standing, sitting or lying down. However, to give full voice they do need to stand up. This remedy helps by restricting vision to prevent the instinctive behaviour being triggered. If necessary a blanket can be partially draped over the travel crate, or window blinds installed in the rear of the car. The latter method is more suited to hot weather conditions, but remember that dogs must not be confined in cars on sunny days. Harnessing the dog at floor level in the vehicle is an alternative to a travel crate, although a less versatile method.

Another possible solution is to use boredom, provided you are endowed with a wealth of patience and resilience. Take your dog only on long car journeys, exceeding fifty miles of uninterrupted motoring. Each journey must be well planned to avoid traffic jams and long delays. Although the start of a journey may be pandemonium, intensifying with every passing minute and mile, a cut-off point is reached, hopefully before the driver's patience becomes exhausted. The dog will eventually become bored and will curl up quietly to dream of more successful hunting forays. This mobile rest method needs reinforcement by continuing the journey for at least another half an hour and repeating long-distance outings on several occasions.

Each subsequent trip should result in the duration of cacophonous behaviour becoming reduced until it does not happen at all. Premature introduction of short journeys by car will, of course, cause the dog to revert to noisy behaviour. Boredom in most training situations is a very negative and non-productive state of affairs. However, in this instance it is a desirable training weapon. Vocal admonishment while the dog is barking only adds to the din and encourages continuation of the unwanted behaviour. It is best to ignore the dog totally throughout remedial journeys.

Unintentional Training

Many dogs are conditioned to become noisy travellers through unintentional training. Regular trips to a venue such as the same park or to training classes may, through associated learning, induce excited barking. During early experiences the dog starts to get excited when nearing the venue; with a few more repetitions his excitement begins the moment he is walked towards the car.

Regular routine does in some circumstances have its drawbacks. To break the association drive several times along the regular route but on arrival at the venue drive straight past.

Gimmick Cures

Expensive scented collars are a modern introduction for curing noisy dogs. A scent cartridge is attached to a special dog collar and when the dog gives voice a small quantity of perfume is discharged. The dog is thus distracted from the inducement causing the barking be-

haviour. One cannot argue with the plausible excuse used to justify the use of this device, as a last resort it is better than euthanasia. However, all that is really necessary to erase the problem is a strong meaningful 'Leave' command and firm supervision.

Another device is the barbaric electric collar, designed to give an electric shock triggered by remote control. I cannot even begin to describe the brutality of this item, the use of which is, in my opinion, completely unjustifiable. Those who employ either the scented or electric collars as therapy should take note: they cause frustration to the wearer, frustration leads to anger, and anger leads to aggression.

SUMMARY
All that is necessary to modify this behaviour, over and above the suggested methods, is the reinforcement of basic control exercises to improve response to the commands 'OK' and 'Leave', which your dog will understand provided they are given with meaning. Remember, if you have to correct three times consecutively for the same sin, you are being too puny.

Commitment in time, effort and purpose is essential when dealing with nuisance barking or any other problem. Being half-hearted is a total waste.

CHAPTER 19

Destructiveness

Chewing Behaviour

Dogs need to chew fibrous materials to clean their teeth, especially when fed on milky and canned products which cause a heavy build-up of plaque. Ideal items for this include garden shrubbery, carpets, newspaper, books, leather, wood, woollen and man-made fibre garments. The unacceptable destructive habit usually begins in puppies as a side-effect of teething, which can be quite painful. Older dogs may suddenly develop a chewing problem through dental decay or gum disease; if not detected in the early stages the habit may continue even after treatment has cleared up the original condition.

Unintentional Training

Misguided custom leads many owners to supply their puppy with a number of toys and take little notice if the pup uses them as teething articles. Unfortunately the puppy is not capable of knowing that it is fine to chew a rubber ball but not the rubber trim on white electrical goods in the utility room, or the difference between a hide chew and a leather handbag. Unintentionally the adult dog has been taught and learned to enjoy destructive chewing as a puppy.

Prevention

Provide your puppy or dog with a clean calf's hoof purchased from your local pet shop. These hooves are real not manmade and by law must be properly cleaned and sterilized before being sold. A calf's hoof comprises compressed cattle hair, which when chewed breaks down into fibre which has a cleansing effect on teeth. To your dog the hoof is totally dissimilar to most other household items and it should be the only article he is allowed to possess. When you see your pup or dog chewing the hoof, reward him with praise.

Try to be tidy and make children put their toys away out of reach of the family pet. Shoes, socks and underwear are highly attractive chew items, surpassed only by reading glasses and spectacle cases. Keeping living areas free of clutter is sound preventive policy, and if your dog does manage to destroy a valued piece of property, you must accept the blame for not putting the item away.

When you catch your dog chewing any item other than the hoof, do not scold him. If you do, any chances of teaching Retrieve are likely to be completely ruined. Instead, take the article using the command 'Thank you' and immediately replace it with the calf's hoof.

Last thing every night give your dog

a biscuit; this routine will imprint the message that it is bed-time and generally lead to undisturbed nights. Also leave the hoof on top of the dog bedding. The prevention policy is based entirely on reward not punishment, and should you be unfortunate enough to discover an article damaged by your dog, scolding him after the event is pointless.

Confinement in a single room has a practical contribution to prevention, and until a puppy can be trusted not to chew household items it should not be given the freedom of the whole house. If the hoof is the only item available when the puppy is confined, it will quickly become the favourite chew toy. Confinement does not mean shutting the dog up in isolation. Playpens are excellent items for puppies, and a baby barrier in the kitchen doorway allows a dog to see all that is going on in the adjacent rooms and to feel part of the pack. The dog may be able to clear a five-foot wall, but is not inclined to leap over a baby barrier.

Learning Not to Chew

When your dog or puppy is in a playful mood, place several household items on the floor in front of him, shoes, slippers, cushion, purse and so on, and include a calf's hoof. If your varmint is true to form he is bound to make a play for an item other than the hoof. The instant he thinks of going for a valued article command 'Leave' and praise compliance with the command. Treat the procedure as a game lasting five or six minutes. Once he has made contact with an article you are too late for the 'Leave' command and must revert to 'Thank you'. When he selects the hoof, praise him enthusiastically.

Within the maximum six-minute period of this game most dogs, especially puppies, become bored and adopt another activity. Make sure you do not miss the moment of decision to stop playing chew; that instant deserves a jackpot reward.

Several repetitions can be made during the game, which should be played twice each day within the twelve-hour memory bank of the dog. Over a period of one to two weeks your dog or puppy will learn that he is not to chew your possessions, in your presence. 'Leave' chew learning must be reinforced with the odd game now and again for a further few weeks.

Vandalism

This usually takes the form of a dog destroying property when he is left on his own.

The scenario begins when the household wakes up; suddenly, after the still of the night, all hell breaks loose. Radio alarms, followed by running cisterns, kettles boiling, the smell of toast and other delightful odours, and residents generally dashing about in great haste. Rover is wound right up by all the action and full of expectation, then, suddenly, the front door closes and he is left with nothing. His whole being screams 'Come back, how can you do this to me?' He must relieve his frustration and immediately attacks any item containing the scent of his owners, cushions, carpet, even the lounge furniture. Gradually he unwinds and rests quietly amongst the debris.

Devastation greets the first person to enter the house. Rover cowers in the corner; not because he knows he has done wrong, but at first because he is demonstrating his aversion to being left out of an imagined hunting foray by the rest of the pack, and subsequently because he has sensed his owner's anger. Either way, admonishment or punishment will not be linked with the crime.

Having a quiet restful five minutes with Rover before leaving home and giving him his breakfast last thing, eliminates the free-fall from maximum excitement to absolute tranquillity when the front door is closed. Leaving a radio on as a familiar background sound can also help.

Rex, a mature dog very easy to live with and well conditioned to enjoying his own company for many hours each working day, has never previously given concern regarding the destruction of material possessions. Until one day his owner returns to find the inside of the front door badly chewed and splintered, curtains destroyed, windows with scored glass and their wooden frames badly damaged. Describing his owner as shocked is an understatement. What happened?

Enquiries to neighbours revealed that a door-to-door salesperson called at the house and was determined to get an answer. Pressing the door chimes was not enough, banging his fist on the front door and peering through a front window for signs of life were the normal preliminaries to his high-pitched sales talk. Poor Rex thought the family den was being attacked and was instinctively driven to defend it. He did his best to get at and drive off the attacking salesman, who, very much amused by events, exacerbated matters by teasing Rex with ever more enthusiastic thumps on the front door until the neighbour intervened. It is difficult to prevent damage in these circumstances. Rex did his job well and, in his mind, went to war fully prepared to lay down his life if need be to preserve the family den.

The risk of such incident is very much reduced if you give all hawkers and deliverers of circulars short shrift when you are at home; the jungle telegraph will quickly transmit the message that calling at your house is a waste of time. Other than this, give some thought to the fact that in the eight to fifteen year life expectancy of your dog the law of probability will bring at least one intruder event, causing severe damage to property. Much can be done to make perimeter doors, fixtures, fittings and furnishings, not only burglar-proof, but dog-proof.

Dog Sitters

People who go out to work all day and leave their dog unsupervised are inviting disaster. The dog may not be destructive when the owners leave the house in the morning, but if they are a few minutes late returning home at the end of the working day the dog may go absolutely crazy with anxiety and relieve his stress with a major bout of destructive chewing. Owners in these circumstances should consider using a dog sitter, which is much more cost effective than referral to a behaviour therapist.

Many retired and elderly people are unable to keep a dog, not because they are no longer active enough, but perhaps because of non-pet property covenants or because of the cost of keeping a dog of their own. They may be lonely, and walking a dog once or twice a day, or having his company during working hours, can be a life-saving exercise for a destructive dog and life-prolonging for the elderly dog minder. Both dog and person are able to fill the void in their lives of social companionship. Keep in mind that your dog sitter is probably saving you a great deal of costly damage, and a small weekly gratuity will help towards the permanency of the arrangement.

Sadly, many so-called caring dog owners treat their dog as a material object, refusing to trust another human being with their dog, preferring to keep their pet in storage until it takes their fancy.

Keeping Trust

Physical punishment, actually striking a dog, damages more than anything else the canine–human relationship. One incident can be enough to erase any trust the dog has in his keeper. This is particularly true with destructive chewing, especially if the punishment is administered after the event.

Many pet dog owners refuse to accept that after the event a dog will not connect punishment with his sin. They are absolutely certain when they arrive home and find damage that their dog knows he has done wrong. It is an indisputable fact that when rewarding, admonishing or punishing a dog, you are doing so to whatever is in the mind of the dog at that exact moment. The correct instant to admonish is when the dog first thinks of chewing a banned article, *before*, not during or after the event. Deviate from this and the depreciation in canine–human trust equals the severity of the punishment.

The Dog's Point of View

Dogs are active creatures, they love life and that means enjoying themselves.

Every dog is also endowed with some degree of mischievousness, which must have an outlet. Too often dogs are left in a situation for long periods of time where the only activity possible is chewing, which then becomes habitual therapy, their release valve from boredom and frustration. The need for relief is so intense that, if punishment was the guaranteed outcome of the crime, nothing short of execution could eradicate the will to repeat the offence.

The worst times of the day for hyperactivity are the two hours immediately following sunrise and the hour preceding sunset. Creatures which are most active at dusk or dawn are referred to as crepuscular. These periods are the most likely times during the day that a dog will do damage and get up to destructive mischief. Everything we do to modify undesirable behaviour has a plus and minus effect. Knowing your dog needs to be exercised to avoid boredom during dawn and dusk periods makes early and late recreational walks seem a good idea. They are, but action increases excitement and consequently the dog must be calmed down on returning home before departing to your place of work. The best exercise for calming a dog and making him relax is the Long Down, and this is an ideal procedure to adopt when you return from an early morning walk.

Regular routine walks affect different dogs in different ways. Only the permanent keeper of the dog can measure the plus and minus effects of the particular routine and how they influence behaviour. Analysing influence on behaviour requires the human partner to think dog! However, thinking in itself is not enough, you have to act dog and be a firm but understanding pack leader.

Kennelling

Folding indoor kennels are an ideal piece of training equipment. Once you have conditioned your dog to using the kennel as his own covered den, you will wonder how you ever managed without it. During the working day, if you have to go out shopping without your dog for about two hours, he will be quite safe and out of harm's way confined in the wire den. On other occasions when you have to drop your level of control, you can slip your dog into the kennel and deal with a phone call, house caller or whatever, in the full knowledge that the freshly roasted Sunday joint on the kitchen work-surface will still be there untouched by canine teeth when you return.

Confinement in the wire den with a calf's hoof and comfortable bedding is in fact a good thing on a regular basis, up to a maximum of two hours each working day. Dogs enjoy the procedure as they are able to relax totally. Periods exceed-ing two hours on a regular basis are unwise as, in time, cumulative frustration through prolonged isolation will induce all sorts of behavioural problems, including aggression. Longer isolation periods when travelling or at family crisis times are permissible, but only on very infrequent occasions.

SUMMARY
Time must be given to teaching your companion that the only item in the home he is allowed to chew is a calf's hoof, and this means playing non-chew training games. You must have the commitment to do what has to be done regarding the education of your dog. Valuable possessions must also be put away when they are finished with.

Finally, with prevention, do not leave until tomorrow changes you should have made yesterday; after the event is too late.

CHAPTER 20

Pulling On Lead

Lead Technique

Some breed types are natural lead dogs, with an inherent trait to surge ahead of their handler. Teaching such a dog to walk comfortably at Heel depends on the correct lead handling technique.

Inexperienced dog owners try to counter-attack the problem by using the heaviest, strongest and shortest lead they can find. When the dog forges ahead, they restrain him by pulling on the lead; the more the handler pulls, the harder the dog pulls. This factor is used during early basic training to reinforce the Stay exercise. Consequently, the heart of the problem is the handler pulling, not the dog. The solution is to teach the human member of the team not to pull and not to follow the offending dog.

The dog must be walked on a slack lead. When taut, it is impossible to administer an effective flick on the lead. Administering the preventive flick requires dexterity on the part of the handler, good timing and a very positive attitude.

The Preventive Flick

The correct Walk at Heel position has the dog's shoulders and right side in line with the left hip of the handler. This is an exact requirement and the preventive flick must be administered when the dog first thinks of losing position, before he gets so much as half a pace ahead of the handler. Timing is the essence of success: flick, slack lead, praise – three actions delivered with the speed of machine-gun fire and without any change of pace on the part of the handler. The flick should not be harsh or forceful, just sudden so that it surprises the dog and switches his mind back to the handler.

Correction is too late and, far from teaching a dog not to forge ahead, reinforces the problem. What usually happens is that the dog swiftly advances five or six paces ahead, his handler pulls hard on the lead, the dog stops momentarily and the handler walks on towards him. The scenario is repeated, and the dog quickly learns that the faster he forges ahead, the quicker his handler will catch him up. This classic example of unintentional training conditions the handler to follow the dog.

Another example of unintentional training is the mother walking her children to school, who thinks it is an ideal opportunity to walk the dog at the same time. She has other things on her mind beside the dog and it does not take many repetitions for her dog to learn the route and become a firm leader, equal to the finest lead sledge dog. Unintentionally, the mother has placed herself in a high human distraction situation not conducive to training her dog properly. Walking to school is fine once the family dog has learned to walk in the at Heel position and once mum has the ability to control her dog.

Concentration and control are the essential factors to success. The handler must have no task or goal in mind other than training the dog and taking one step at a time without losing control.

Other Interventions

As well as the preventive flick on the lead, there are other surprises you can use to control your dog, such as the compelled Auto Sit, or Circles Left and Right. You must also have the commitment necessary to be stronger willed than a stubborn dog. When your dog decides to go right, you must go left; if he forges ahead turn sharply and go as fast as you can in the opposite direction. Repeat these tactics again and again if necessary, until your dog pays attention and respects your wishes. Your dog cannot charge ahead unless you allow him to do so.

At Heel Concentration

Making a dog pay attention and concentrate on what his handler is doing has to be imprinted gradually, with distraction increased a little at a time. If he cannot be made to Walk at Heel on his tag lead indoors, he is not likely to do so in high distraction situations outdoors. Other indoor training includes the hands-off lead around waist procedure, the lead acting as a physical and mental cord. Mental communication is reinforced by ignoring the dog, and by taking advantage of canine pack instinct to be in close harmony and favour with the pack leader.

Once your dog conforms properly on the

home patch, including the garden, more adventurous locations can be found and barriers introduced into the learning procedures which make it difficult for him to move ahead of you. Walking against the flow of pedestrian traffic in shopping centres compels your dog to watch where he is going and to think. With a little luck, he will quickly realize that you are more skilled than he is at selecting a smooth passage through the crowds of people.

Another excellent training tool is the grid, made up from 6ft (1.8m) lengths of 1in (2.5cm) wood batten. The battens are laid on the ground parallel to each other at 12in (30cm) intervals to form an oblong grid about 12ft by 6ft (3.6m by 1.8m). The dog is set facing the right-hand corner of the grid and walked anticlockwise around the perimeter. The handler is able to walk on level ground, but the dog has to pick his way over the battens, having to think where to put his feet and concentrate. All thoughts of dashing forward are diluted by the need to focus attention on the task in hand. Add really sincere motivating praise and the problem is solved.

Gimmicks

Water pistols are sometimes suggested as a means of discouraging pulling on lead. Each time the dog puts his nose too far ahead, his handler gives him a short squirt, he is surprised and drops back to Heel position. Although some behaviour patterns can be learned in a single experience using a shock followed by reward method, in this particular instance if the dog realizes the handler is squirting the water he will learn to keep his distance, not to Walk at Heel. Water pistols are therefore a gimmick which induce an unpleasant association with heelwork. The object of the learning exercise is to give your dog a pleasant association with walking close to you, and to this end praise is the principal training tool.

Head collars are another gimmick control device. They are alleged to be a modern development, but in fact figure-of-eight collars have been in use for well over 150 years. These collars are designed to fit over the muzzle and head of a dog, and they provide a means of physical control in circumstances where handler discipline, empathy with and control of the dog need to be reinforced. Such collars are a poor substitute for essential handler leadership and power of command. They do, however, have a place in the dog world, in situations where temporary control is needed, such as when an aggressive dog has to be examined by a veterinarian or other clinician.

Close Communication

Walking at Heel is a close-to-handler requirement, and vocal commands play an important part in the dog understanding what his handler requires. Using the three Rs, we will Research an example of lead pulling.

Rover treats his owner as an inanimate lump of porridge, a burden to be towed as fast as possible to locations which his nose determines are the most worthy of investigation. Given open space and a decent lead length Rover can shoot off in any direction. He is mentally oblivious of his handler; sounds, sight and scent inducements within the immediate environment fully occupy his mind. Hence, the problem, distraction, is Recognized.

The Remedy is to make the handler a

bigger distraction than the environment. Before embarking on a programme of training sessions to modify the undesired behaviour, some armchair thinking and analysis of all that is involved must be carried out, especially with regard to technique. Consideration should be given to direct and indirect strategies. The indirect concern such questions as whether the dog has been played with enough in the past, and whether the dog is bored by his owner or finds him interesting. The direct strategy concerns creating circumstances where the only physical option is for the dog to stay close at Heel, and to remove all other options. Also, any basic exercises which the dog is good at may help as a foundation for new learning, 'Stay' or Entry-Exit discipline perhaps. Finally the likely negative side-effects to the intended strategy should be considered. A dog using his nose and forging ahead on a search or tracking exercise is desirable, thus the trait must not be totally erased.

Indirect Measures

Indirect measures require reinforcing basic training with more static exercises to reduce excitement: playing tug-of-war and always winning; rewarding the conclusion of all successful exercises with play using a toy; playing with a frisbee during recreational outings; preparing the dog's dinner before taking him for a walk and feeding him immediately on returning home. All these tactics have the positive effect of enhancing the affinity of a dog with his handler.

One other indirect tactic is twice a day when you are sitting down make your dog face you and gently pet him about the head and ears. Place a titbit on your left knee and allow your dog to take it; keep tapping your left thigh with your hand to indicate the location of the titbit. Repetition of this over a period of time will imprint a happy association. Consequently, tapping your left thigh when training him to Walk at Heel can be a very motivating learning tool.

Direct Measures

Direct methods which prevent undesirable options during practical training include using the correct on-lead control position with just 2in (5cm) of slack lead to inhibit lagging and forging; walking the dog against a good length of straight wall which prevents evasive movements to the left; and holding an object of attraction such as a favourite toy in the left hand and just out of his reach.

Commands already learned, such as 'Wait', 'Steady' and 'Stay', can be useful as timely interventions. New commands which can be purposeful include 'Close', given in a very cheerful motivating tone of voice. When changing direction to the left the command 'Back' is very effective. Teach 'Back' through a series of on-the-spot Circles Left, substituting the 'Back' command for 'Dog's name, Heel'.

When all else fails, a titbit every five or six paces while slow pacing a hungry dog may fully occupy the offender's mind and make the handler the biggest distraction in the world. Gradually the frequency of titbits can be reduced and eventually stopped.

SUMMARY

Your goal must be to make your left knee a most attractive place of comfort and interest for your dog. Take matters one step at a time, both in the practical and strategic sense. Make sure your chosen method will not have the opposite effect to what you intend; this takes concentration, the ability to read your dog and to think ahead of him.

Finally, do not rush with the distraction level, make progress a little at a time. First settle for ten perfect Walk at Heel paces without having to use any intervention. The first time you achieve this, be ready with a reward. Next make fifteen paces your goal, then twenty, and so on up to fifty paces including changes of direction. Achieve this and you will have a dog that is a pleasure to take for walks.

CHAPTER 21

Jumping Up

The dog who has been conditioned to respond properly to 'Sit' or 'Down' cannot jump up and comply with the command at the same time.

Unintentional Training

Most dogs develop the habit of jumping up when they are puppies; members of the family greet their new puppy by picking up what they believe to be a lovely bundle of fluff to cuddle and comfort at face level. No account is given to the subsequent dog behaviour that will become established when the dog is fully grown.

You may not be too bothered when your dog jumps up on your working clothes, but will be angry when he does the same to your evening dress, usually when he has muddy feet and is slobbering. Your dog is indifferent to what you are wearing; lines of demarcation between allowing or not allowing are grey areas beyond the understanding of a canine mind. Defensive evasive responses on your part tend to make matters worse and trigger your dog to try harder to make enthusiastic contact.

Some unintentional or accidental canine misbehaviour can be self-inflicted on the owner's part. The classic example is not to go to Crufts in a fur coat. With several thousand dogs in location on any one day of the show, you run the risk of numerous dogs wishing to use you as a retrieve article.

Remedy

The best remedy is to ignore the dog who jumps up. Being ignored deprives the dog of any possible reward, and he will then adopt other patterns of behaviour to attract your attention. When you come home to your dog walk straight past him without even making eye contact, keep moving swiftly and side-step any attempts on his part to make contact with you. Only when your dog has spent his initial excitement and settled down should you take notice by making him obey two or three commands. Through this you will gain the necessary level of control to block the undesired jumping-up behaviour.

Human instinct makes it difficult to ignore a highly active dog; it seems only natural to look at him and fend him off. Try to see things from the dog's point of view though; after a short period of separation your dog will interpret any response from you as a reward. Actual hand contact gives him a huge pleasurable reward, while speaking to him or even giving the command 'Sit' makes him think 'Wonderful, I'm noticed'. This does not contradict the advice to ignore, as the command would come before you reach the entrance, before the dog becomes over-excited. If someone else is in the house, they can command the dog to 'Sit' and supervise events during your arrival.

Physical Correction

Heavy physical correction, such as thumping the dog in the chest with your knee, is not a good idea. Such treatment does absolutely nothing to enhance a trusting relationship.

Mild physical correction is useful in circumstances where an excited dog being Walked at Heel on-lead jumps up at his handler every five or six paces, a favourite habit of herding breed types of dog. The habit can be erased by the handler using his left hand as a sliding clutch on the lead which is held in the control position. The instant the dog tries to jump up, the left hand is clamped tight on the lead with the arm fully extended downwards towards the dog, leaving the elbow unbent. In practice this takes less than a fraction of a second and the dog is taken by surprise and comes to a sudden stop in mid-flight. Two or three repetitions are usually sufficient for him to realize that leaping-up behaviour is not a good idea. Breeds prone to arthritis in the neck, such as the Doberman, should not be subjected to sliding clutch lead corrections.

Another mild physical method is to step sideways to the left across the dog's path at the exact instant he commences the upward leap. This requires good timing.

The handler must keep moving without any change in pace for both these physical interventions. If the dog ends up with his right front paw over the lead do not bend down to adjust matters, let the dog sort his own foot out. It is different, however, if there is a double turn round the leg; this must be immediately corrected as the dog could easily break a leg.

Persistent offenders usually respond to the 'Gay Gordons' technique. Hold the dog's two front feet when he is standing on his hind legs and, without making any eye contact, waltz him backwards and forwards. The feet must be held firmly but not squeezed, keeping him up on his hind legs for a good half a minute. Combine this with ignoring him other than to admonish any attempt to mouth your hands, and your success is guaranteed after one or two repetitions.

Regression

Your best efforts can be undermined and the dog regress back to his old ways if other members of the household fail to treat him the same way you do. Counter-conditioning an undesirable canine habit becomes progressively harder after each regression. Commitment to training not only the family dog, but all other human members of the household, is essential.

Casual visitors can also undermine your best efforts. When your dog jumps up at them or uses his nose vigorously to smell their clothing, your command of 'Dog's name, Leave' is usually met with 'It's all right, I don't mind. I like dogs.' If you accept this and cannot be bothered to intervene and prevent the behaviour, two months later you will be wondering why you no longer have any visitors. Can you then blame your dog?

CHAPTER 22

Separation Anxiety

Over-Socialization

Dogs who become over-socialized with their owners suffer separation anxiety when left alone. The condition can be so acute that the owner leaving for just a few seconds causes the dog severe anxiety. The hurt is not only mentally traumatic, it is physically painful; howling, destructive chewing, and digging can be continuous until the owner returns. Severe cases will even chew their own coats and skin, inflicting on themselves horrendous weeping lesions of eczema.

Causes

It is often the case that too much affection has been shown to a puppy. A human–puppy relationship begun on the terms of love at first sight wanes as the pup matures; conditioned to total dependence on human company, the puppy finds the reduction in social contact difficult to cope with.

Similar problems occur with older dogs who have been re-homed, especially if they come from rescue kennels. Adult rescue dogs take about eight weeks to become confident and show their true character in a new home. How they are treated during that time can have a considerable influence on the ultimate behaviour of the dog.

Dominance

Anxious dogs often become hyperdominant over their owners and display extreme protective behaviour. They want to control all events in the day-to-day routine of family life. Members of the household find they are not allowed to go to the bathroom without being escorted and supervised by the dog. If this dog is left in the kitchen at bedtime the whole community will suffer a sleepless night due to his noisy behaviour. Natural necessity works in reverse in this instance; the human victim in the relationship relents by admitting the dog to the bedroom and eventually the owner is only allowed on the bed with the dog's consent.

Prevention

The benefits of the ignoring strategy with a canine newcomer to the household have been well explained in previous chapters. Over-familiarity during the early weeks of a new human–dog relationship is definitely counter-productive. Right from the very start, a balanced programme of socialization and isolation must be maintained; too little or too much of either can be disastrous.

Two hours of total isolation each working day is the correct balance for teaching your dog to enjoy his own company. Low ceiling height and two doors between him and any other creature are essential to isolation, and indoor folding kennels are ideal pieces of equipment. In addition, when you wish to put your feet up or watch television you can move the kennel to the perimeter of the room and put your dog in it, which has the bonus of teaching him that he is lower in rank than the other pack members.

Total isolation in excess of two hours each working day will, in time, cause a variety of behavioural problems. However, when conditioned to the kennel your dog can be isolated overnight, but the door should be left open. Night hours do not count towards social isolation.

Social contact during the early weeks of the relationship must be purposeful and take the form of fifteen to thirty minutes of social grooming each day. The combination of isolation and social grooming strikes the right balance of familiarity and dependence. Other than this every activity during the working day must be at the instigation of the owner not the dog.

Desensitizing

Dogs suffering from established separation anxiety cannot immediately be isolated in a kennel for two hours, but need to undergo a programme of very gradual desensitizing. They can, though, be kennelled in close proximity and in sight of their owner. Distance can gradually be increased over two or three weeks until eventually, when the dog is at rest, the owner can remain out of sight for some time. Impatience or over-confidence may encourage you to progress too quickly. Thoroughness is the priority and desensitization must be a very slow procedure if it is to be successful.

During the first two or three weeks of this programme, if the dog plays up during brief absences when you go to the bathroom, kitchen and so on, it is best to ignore him. Under no circumstances must he be admonished; any attention will, of course, reward the undesired behaviour.

Common sense will dictate when the time is right to begin the total isolation routine. Again, the duration of two hours must be built up in slow increments starting with ten minutes, then twenty, and so on. Care must be taken not to release the dog from isolation when he is being noisy. It does not hurt occasionally to give the kennelled dog a titbit when he is quiet, but the presentation of the treat must be matter-of-fact and any words kept very curt.

Counter-Conditioning

The fact that dogs learn by association can be put to good effect by using a counter-conditioning agent which is associated with the owner. An old cardigan containing the owner's scent is ideal for this, and background music or television are also agents which help to comfort the dog during long absences.

Unintentional Training

Some owners are in the position of being able to take their dogs to work each day. On face value this is excellent, but consider the long-term effects. During the eight to fifteen year life expectancy of a dog, circumstances may change and it may become impossible to take the dog to work; he will then have to be left at home all day and probably not take kindly to the sudden change in his way of life. Despite the best of intentions, the dog has become conditioned to expect too much and take matters for granted. Problems are much less likely to occur if he has been conditioned to enjoy his own company through a balanced isolation programme.

Forward thinking and planning are needed for such breaks in routine as annual holidays. Who will look after your dog while you are away? If he has to go into boarding kennels, his place must be reserved months before your holiday date. Give some thought to his feelings; even if you have spent the time to desensitize separation anxiety, he will still need a programme of pre-conditioning to kennel life before you can board him and take off for two or more weeks. Arrange for the kennels to take him for an odd day now and again for just two hours at a time, then in easy stages from a day, a day and a night, building up to a long weekend. Your dog will then know that you will come back for him and will not totally regress while you are away. Better still, give up foreign holidays and take him with you. If treated right, your dog will not only be a best friend, but the best dog in the whole world.

Chauvinism

People usually associate chauvinism with a dominant male attitude to females. The divorce rate in modern times has exploded numerically, a sure sign that generally standards of behaviour and tolerance are not what they used to be. Lowering standards of moral behaviour have an effect on family dogs. Every holiday season hundreds of dogs are dumped by selfish people who realize at the last moment that they cannot take their dogs on a Continental holiday. Another classic example is unthinking people who buy pets as Christmas presents, leading perhaps to a puppy going to an owner who does not want it and who discards it with no more consideration than they give kitchen waste.

Dogs are for life, and they have feelings which can be easily hurt. Some adorable puppies end up being re-homed several times during their first year of life in this less than perfect world. Repetitive rejection can in the long term totally prevent any possibility of pack security being established in the dog's mind. Some dogs are, of course, mentally bullet-proof, but those who are endowed with a strong pack instinct really do suffer and, when or if they find a permanent home, endure acute separation anxiety.

The soundest piece of canine advice I can possibly give is for whatever reason you think you have to buy a dog, think again and think ahead.

Conclusion

'Tis not in mortals to command success, But we'll do more, Sempronius; we'll deserve it.

Joseph Addison (1672–1719)

Learning to train a dog from books leaves a lot to be desired. There are no short cuts. Hopefully, this book will enable novice owners to avoid many classic mistakes and experienced dog people to review and add to their knowledge.

Thirty or more volumes of encyclopaedia could not contain everything there is to know about dogs. A little success sometimes motivates a thirst for further achievement and knowledge. When it does so, you become bitten by the bug and embark on a fascinating and absorbing hobby, perhaps even a career. Should just one reader through this book find that initial degree of success to improved canine understanding, then my writing will have been worth while. Another bonus may be that many intending owners who do not have the time to give the necessary commitment will defer the responsibility of dog ownership until their circumstances allow the obligation.

Making a student dog handler think broadly enough regarding each basic exercise is one of the most difficult things either in writing or in any other format. For example the main purpose in Walk at Heel training is to establish a bond, a relationship between handler and dog, to make the Heel position a place of refuge and comfort for the dog and the starting-point for mental communication.

The most common handler mistake is, without doubt, selecting the wrong dog or puppy in the first place. Dogs, as well as people, have personality traits which must be considered. There is no excuse for misplacements as experienced aptitude testers are available. Equally important, they are able to assess the suitability of potential puppy or dog owners.

If you are anticipating dog ownership, do use the services of an independent dog person able to make the selection for you, who should supply a written report of the puppy or dog personality profile and, in the case of a pedigree breed purchase, ensure that all the paperwork is in order: Kennel Club Registration, signed pedigree chart, diet sheet and bill of sale with impartial protective clauses for breeder and client. Sudden impulse to become a dog owner stands more than a fifty-fifty chance of becoming a catastrophic disaster. Do sit down and really think about what you are taking on. Let common sense guide your decision and take heed of a slightly modified barrack room quotation: 'proper planning and preparation prevent poor performance'. Hopefully, you will then achieve the *status quo* of being a team, your dog and you together, working and living with, not just for each other.

Index